My God

Is So Great!

62 Games
to Help Preschoolers
Know and Love God

Group
Loveland, Colorado

MY GOD IS SO GREAT!
Copyright © 1999 Group Publishing, Inc.

Visit our Web site: www.grouppublishing.com

Credits
Contributing Authors: Chip Borgstadt, Katy Borgstadt, Robin Christy, Jacqui Dunham, Karen R. Humphrey, Carol Mader, Janet Miller, and Carol Smith
Editor: Jody Brolsma
Creative Development Editor: Dave Thornton
Chief Creative Officer: Joani Schultz
Copy Editor: Pamela Shoup
Designer and Art Director: Jean Bruns
Computer Graphic Artist: Anita Cook
Cover Art Director: Jeff A. Storm
Cover Designer: Andrea L. Boven
Cover Illustrator: Susan Calitri
Illustrator: Nancy Munger
Production Manager: Peggy Naylor

Library of Congress Cataloging-in-Publication Data
My God is so great! : 62 games to help preschoolers know and love God.
    p.   cm.
    Includes index.
    ISBN 0-7644-2094-1 (alk. paper)
    1. Christian education of preschool children. 2. God—Attributes-Study and teaching (Preschool) 3. God—Biblical teaching—Study and teaching (Preschool) 4. Games in Christian education.
    I. Group Publishing.
    BV1475.8.M8 1999   99-21480
    268'.432—dc21   CIP

10 9 8 7 6 5 4 3 2 1   08 07 06 05 04 03 02 01 00 99

Printed in the United States of America.

Contents

Introduction

"God is great. God is good. Now we thank him for this food."

"Jesus loves me! This I know, for the Bible tells me so..."

"My God is so great, so strong and so mighty! There's nothing my God cannot do!"

These simple lines of song and prayer are the beginnings of a child's knowledge of God. Preschoolers, in particular, are new in their faith and understanding of the nature of God. They may not have had the opportunity to see prayers faithfully answered. They don't have the knowledge of science that makes God's creation so remarkable to us. Most children haven't experienced the humility and wonder of God's awesome forgiveness. And they haven't even begun to see God's hand, graciously and generously giving every perfect gift.

What precious, tender soil you have before you! That's why *My God Is So Great!* was created—to give you the seeds to plant in children's hearts, guiding them in a better understanding of their Heavenly Father. Each activity, game, or song will open children's eyes to one of God's character traits. Use these ideas to supplement your own lessons, or use several of them to create an entire lesson on each character trait. The experienced authors have added "Preschool Play Pointers" to give ideas for extending an activity or to provide age-level insights that ensure meaningful learning. Children will love playing, singing, and moving while they learn more about God. And you'll be delighted to see children develop a clearer understanding of their Heavenly Father.

The children in your class are about to get a better picture of Go—a God who is loving, wise, regal, gracious, mighty, and creative. Before you begin, pray that children's eyes might be opened, that their hearts will be touched, and that their lives will be eternally changed. Thank you for investing yourself in the lives of children. Your love and care will give them a glimpse of God.

GOD IS
All-Knowing

"Oh, the depth of the riches
of the wisdom and knowledge of God!
How unsearchable his judgments,
and his paths beyond tracing out!"
(Romans 11:33)

Which Hand?

GROWING CLOSER: God knows all about us.

KEY VERSE: "For God is greater than our hearts, and he knows everything" (1 John 3:20b).

SUPPLIES: A small eraser or other object for each child. Objects must be small enough for children to conceal in one fist.

The Game:

Say: **This is a guessing game that you may have played with your mom or dad, or maybe with a brother or sister.** Put your hands behind your back, and hide the eraser in one hand. Then bring your closed fists forward and allow children to take turns guessing which hand holds the eraser by tapping one of your hands.

Then say: **This is a guessing game— we never know how it will turn out.** Give each child an eraser and say: **Take turns playing the guessing game with a partner until I clap my hands two times.** After one minute, clap your hands, and have children set down the erasers.

Preschool PLAY POINTER

When selecting small items, be sure they aren't smaller than a fifty-cent piece. Very small items may be a choking hazard for younger preschoolers.

Ask: • **How well did you do at guessing which hand held the eraser?**

• **How did you know which hand to tap?**

• **What other things do we have to guess about?**

Say: **We have to guess about a lot of things in life, because we don't ever know how things are going to turn out. You might wonder what kind of job you'll have when you grow up or what you'll get for Christmas. But God never has to guess. God always knows how things will turn out. When we wake up in the morning, God already knows how our day will turn out.**

Put your hands behind your back, and hide your eraser in one of your hands. Pause while children follow your instructions. **I don't know which hand you put your eraser in, but God knows. He always knows how things will turn out. God knows everything. Hold out your hand that's holding**

the eraser, and we'll pray and thank God for knowing all about us.

Pray: **Dear God, we're glad that you know everything. You know what will happen to us and how our lives will turn out. Thank you for watching over us and knowing all about us. Amen.**

Shoe Scramble

GROWING CLOSER: God knows us.
KEY VERSE: "O Lord, you have searched me and you know me" (Psalm 139:1).
SUPPLIES: a Bible, one large carpet square, masking tape

The Game:

Before children arrive, use the masking tape to make a circle large enough so that all the children can sit around it. Place a large carpet square in the center of the circle.

Have children sit on the masking tape line, with their legs stretched out in front of them. Say: **Look at all the different shoes we're wearing!**

Ask: • **How are your shoes different from other children's shoes?** Children may respond that some shoes are brown and others are black, or that some shoes tie with laces and others have buckles.

Say: **Everyone is wearing nice shoes, but they're all a little different. Let's take off our shoes to play a game.**

As children are removing their shoes, say: **Our different shoes remind me of the way God made each of us. We're all different in many ways, but God knows each of us very well.** Have children place their shoes in a pile in the center of the circle. When all the shoes are in the center of the circle, mix them up.

Then say: **Now we're going to see how well you know your own shoes. On the count of three, go to the middle of the circle, and find your own shoes. Ready? One, two, three!** If you have more than ten children, you may want to call on three or four children at a time. Or call all the children who are wearing white socks, children who ate cereal for breakfast, or children who have a pet dog.

After children have found their own shoes, ask then to put

the shoes on their feet. You may need to help children fasten their shoes. While children are getting their shoes on, ask:

- **How did you find your shoes?**
- **How did you know that these were your shoes?**

Say: **Since we wear our shoes all the time, we can see what makes our shoes different from others. God made each of us different in many ways, too.**

Ask: • **How are you different from other children in this class?**

Say: **The Bible tells us that God knows us very well.** Read aloud Psalm 139:1 from an easy-to-understand Bible translation. **God loves us and knows everything about us because he made us. He gave us our hair, our skin, our eyes, and even our fingerprints. God knows everything about us. Just as you could pick your shoes from the pile, God knows you well enough to find you in a crowd of people. Instead of clapping, let's stomp our feet to celebrate the fact that God knows us and loves us!**

Lead children in a "stomping ovation"!

A Human Knot

GROWING CLOSER: God knows how to help us.
KEY VERSE: "Then Peter came to himself and said, 'Now I know without a doubt that the Lord sent his angel and rescued me from Herod's clutches'" (Acts 12:11a).
SUPPLIES: none

The Game:

Have children form a circle, standing shoulder to shoulder and facing in. Say: **Put one arm straight out in front of your body. Now, take hold of the hand of someone standing across from you. Don't let go of each other's hands, and don't squeeze hands too hard.** If there's an odd number of children, join the circle and hold a child's hand. **Now, put your other arm into the circle straight out in front of you. Take hold of another person's hand. Hold the hand of a different person than you did the first time.** Help children find another hand to hold.

Ask: • **What do you think we've just made?**

• **While your arms are still tangled up, what might happen if you tried to walk across the room?**

Say: **Let's see if you can take one step together. You'll need to be very slow and careful so no one falls over or gets hurt. When I count to three, everybody take one little step towards the door. Ready? One, two, three, step.**

Help children take one little step. Guide them in taking several slow, careful steps together.

Ask: • **What is it like to move with your hands all in a knot?**

Say: **Now we're going to pretend each of you is Peter, a man in the Bible. Peter was chained up inside the prison, with guards on both sides of him. He could move only a little bit, just as you can move only a little since you're all joined together. Peter was stuck, but God is all-knowing, and God knew how to help Peter. Peter's friends prayed and asked for God's help. Then God sent an angel who touched Peter and woke him up. Suddenly, the chains fell off and Peter was free!** Have children drop hands. **The angel led Peter out of the prison, past all the guards, and none of them even saw him!**

Ask: • **What can you do, now that your hands are free?**

Say: **When we have a problem, sometimes we can feel stuck, just as you were with your hands all tied up. But God knows everything—he knows how to untangle our problems and set us free! Let's clap and praise God for knowing all about us and our problems!** Lead children in clapping for God.

God's Eyes

GROWING CLOSER: God can see things that we can't see.

KEY VERSE: "The angel said to the women, 'Do not be afraid, for I know that you are looking for Jesus...He is not here; he has risen, just as he said' " (Matthew 28:5-6a).

SUPPLIES: classroom objects such as chairs and tables, scarves (optional)

The Game:

Set up a simple obstacle course that winds around the class-room. The course can go over children's chairs, under tables, and around play areas.

Have children close their eyes.

Ask: • **What do you see?**

• **What things are hard to do with your eyes closed?**

Allow children to open their eyes. Say: **When our eyes are closed, we can't see what's happening around us. We have to trust people whose eyes are open. Let's play a game to see what that's like.** Have children form pairs, then use a scarf to blindfold one child in each pair.

Instruct the sighted partner to lead the blindfolded partner through the obstacle course, using gentle actions and words. When partners reach the end of the course, allow them to trade roles and move through the course again. Then collect the scarves, and ask:

Preschool
PLAY POINTER

Be sensitive to the fact that some younger preschoolers might not like to be blindfolded. Allow those children to simply close their eyes or put their hands over their eyes.

• **What was it like to be blindfolded?**

• **How did you know where to go?**

Say: **In this game, your partner could see things that you couldn't see. God is like that too. Sometimes there are things that we can't see, like what will happen in our lives, who our friends will be, or when someone will get well. Since God knows everything, we have to trust that God will help us get through scary or hard times.**

The Bible tells us about the time that Jesus, God's Son, died. Jesus' friends were sad—that's because they didn't know what God knew! God knew that Jesus would rise from the dead.

Lead children through the obstacle course again. As children walk through the course, have them chant, "God can see! God can see!"

Questions, Questions

GROWING CLOSER: God can answer all of our questions.

KEY VERSE: "Ask and it will be given to you; seek and you will find; knock and the door will be opened to you" (Matthew 7:7).

SUPPLIES: none

The Game:

Use this creative prayer to help children verbalize their questions and concerns to God.

Say: **You are a bunch of smart children! I'll bet you know lots and lots of things.**

• **What are some things you know?** Children may respond that they know how to count to fifty or that they know their colors or letters. Applaud children for even the simplest things they've learned. Then continue: **Even though we know lots of things, there are still many things we don't know. You may wonder why you have to get sick sometimes or why God made the sky blue and not orange.**

Ask: • **Who might be able to answer all of your questions?**

Say: **Moms or dads or teachers can answer some questions, but God knows the answer to all of our questions. There's a song we can sing when we have questions to ask God.**

Lead children in the following song, to the tune of "God Is So Good."

God knows it all.
God knows it all.
I am so glad
That God knows it all.

Call on a few children to voice their questions, then sing the song again as a reminder that God knows the answers to all of our questions.

Preschool PLAY POINTER

You may want to explain that God answers many of our questions in the Bible. If time allows, sing the song again, substituting the word "tells" for "knows." Help children understand that the Bible is our "answer book" from God.

Future Dance

GROWING CLOSER: God knows how things will turn out.

KEY VERSE: " 'For I know the plans I have for you,' declares the Lord, 'plans to prosper you and not to harm you, plans to give you hope and a future' " (Jeremiah 29:11).

SUPPLIES: motion cards (p. 13), audiocassette of children's praise music, cassette player

The Game:

Before children arrive, photocopy and cut apart the motion cards on page 13. (If you have more than six children, photocopy two sets of cards.) Cue a lively praise song on the cassette player.

Hold up the motion cards and say: **In this game, each person will have a chance to turn over a card. The cards tell us what motions to do to the music—clapping, jumping, touching the ground, turning around, waving our arms, or marching. First, let's try to guess which card will come up last.** Let each child make a guess, then start the music.

Have one child draw a card and lead others in doing that action for a few seconds. While children are still performing the action, call up another child to draw a new card. Continue the "dance" until the last card is drawn. Then gather children and ask:

• **Who guessed the card that was last?**

• **How did you know that would be the last card?**

Say: **When we try to predict things, we're sometimes wrong. That's because we can really only guess. But God is never wrong. God knows everything! God knows how things will turn out. We can trust that God knows what's going to happen, even when we don't. And that might make us feel like doing a dance!**

You may want to play the game again, allowing children to move and dance as they praise God for his wisdom.

Motion Cards

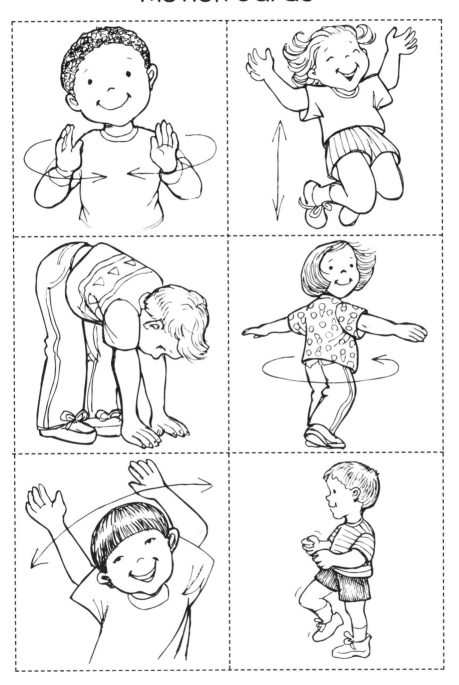

GOD IS
Creative

"You are worthy,

our Lord and God,

to receive glory and honor and power,

for you created all things,

and by your will they were created

and have their being."

(Revelation 4:11)

Creation Dance

GROWING CLOSER: God made everything.

KEY VERSE: "The God who made the world and everything in it is the Lord of heaven and earth and does not live in temples built by hands" (Acts 17:24).

SUPPLIES: a drum or rhythm instrument

The Game:

Ask • **What wonderful things did God make?**

Say: **God made everything you see in nature. He made the highest mountains and the lowest valleys. God made the sun, the clouds, and the rivers. God made *everything*, and we're going to learn a dance to celebrate what God has made. First, here are the motions we'll use.**

Teach children the following motions:

MOUNTAINS: Walk on tiptoes while touching your fingertips together to create a "peak" over your head.

VALLEYS: Bend over and walk, clasping your hands below you to form a V.

CLOUDS: Wiggle your fingers above your head.

SUN: Touch the tips of your fingers together to form a circle overhead.

RIVERS: Put your hands close together, palms facing each other, and wiggle them from side to side.

Gather in a circle, and have someone beat the drum slowly and rhythmically. Lead children in walking in a circle, taking one step on each drumbeat. Then chant these words, while leading children in the motions:

> **God made the mountains.** *(Walk to the right, with hands "peaked" overhead.)*
>
> **God made the valleys.** *(Walk to the right, and lean over with hands making a "valley.")*
>
> **God made the clouds up in the sky.** *(Stop walking, turn around in place, and make swirling motions overhead.)*
>
> **God made the sun that shines so warm.** *(Face into the circle, and make a "sun" overhead.)*
>
> **God made the rivers.** *(Wiggle hands, and walk toward the middle of the circle.)*
>
> **God made you and I.** *(Join hands, and crouch down.)*

Thank you, God! *(Stand up, still holding hands.)*

Lead children in the Creation Dance several times, then pray together. Let children thank God for different parts of creation.

Unexpected Surprises

Preschool
PLAY POINTER

Let children take turns beating the drum. As children become more familiar with the motions, encourage them to create new motions for other things God created, such as animals, flowers, or stars.

GROWING CLOSER: God uses people to do unexpected things.

KEY VERSE: "Andrew, Simon Peter's brother, spoke up, 'Here is a boy with five small barley loaves and two small fish, but how far will they go among so many?' ...Jesus then took the loaves, gave thanks, and distributed to those who were seated as much as they wanted. He did the same with the fish" (John 6:8-9,11).

SUPPLIES: a Bible, cotton balls, plastic spoons, kitchen tongs, cups, tweezers, or other items which children can use to carry the cotton balls

The Game:

Before children arrive, place the cotton balls in a pile at one end of the room. Set the extra items on a table, near the cotton balls.

Say: **Let's see how many ways we can carry these cotton balls to the other side of the room, without touching them with our hands. I've brought lots of other things that you can use.** As preschoolers think of ways to move the cotton balls, let them try their ideas. Children may think of picking up the cotton balls with tongs or tweezers, pinching the cotton balls between their toes, blowing the cotton balls, or scooping the balls into a cup. After everyone has tried at least one idea, ask:

• **What did you think when I told you that you couldn't use your hands?**

• **How does your face look when you're surprised by something?**

Say: **Just as we tried different ways to move cotton balls, God sometimes does things differently, too. Listen to the surprising way that Jesus fed a huge crowd.**

Read aloud John 6:5-14 from an easy-to-understand Bible translation. (Since this is a long story for preschoolers, you may read it from a picture Bible or Bible storybook.)

Ask: • **What would you think if Jesus asked for your lunch to help feed a big crowd?**

Say: **God is creative—he may do things differently, but God's ways always work! Just as God used the little boy to help feed a big crowd, God can use you or me to do amazing and wonderful things.**

Making Rain

GROWING CLOSER: God made different kinds of weather.
KEY VERSE: "I will send rain on the earth" (Genesis 7:4b).
SUPPLIES: none

The Game:

Gather children in a circle, and say: **We know that God made everything with his own hands. God even made the rain! Let's pretend it's raining. We can't make real rain with our hands, only God can do that. But we *can* use our hands to make the sound of a rainstorm. Just follow what I do.** Lead children in the following actions to create the sound of a rainstorm. Do each action for about fifteen seconds.

Rub thumbs and index fingers together. Say: **It's just beginning to sprinkle.**
Hold your palms together and drum your fingers against each other. Say: **Now it's beginning to rain.**
Clap hands softly. Say: **The rain is falling a little harder now.**
Clap hands loudly. Say: **The rain is falling hard.**
Pat hands on knees. Say: **Wow! It's really starting to come down!**
Pound hands on the floor. Say: **This really sounds like a storm!**
Reverse the steps to make the "rain" stop. Say: **That was quite a rainstorm!**
Ask: • **Why do we need rain?**
• **What would happen if it didn't rain?**

Preschool PLAY POINTER

Although many adults may have done this activity before, remember that it's new and exciting to the preschoolers in your class. Allow them to experience the delight in hearing the "rainstorm" right in their own room!

Say: **The Bible tells us that all God had to do was say a word and things were created! God could have said, "Rain," and it would start to rain. God made everything. He created the rain to give us water and to make the plants grow. Even though we had fun making rain sounds, God is the only one who can make rain.**

Unique Boutique

GROWING CLOSER: God made us each different.
KEY VERSE: "I praise you because I am fearfully and wonderfully made; your works are wonderful, I know that full well" (Psalm 139:14).
SUPPLIES: a Bible, dress-up clothes, such as oversized shirts, T-shirts, large shoes, silly hats, neckties, dresses

The Game:

Say: **Today we are going to play an exciting dress-up game to learn more about how God created each one of us in a wonderful and special way.** Help the children form groups of three. Place the dress-up clothes in the center of the room, and have the groups stand about ten- to fifteen-feet away from the clothes.

Say: **There are enough dress-up clothes here to make everyone look goofy and silly. To play this game, first decide which person in your group has the shortest hair.** Pause while children choose the person with the shortest hair. Continue: **When I say "go," the person with the shortest hair will run to the pile of clothes and choose two things to wear. That person will put those two pieces of clothing on, then run back and tag someone else to come and put on two new pieces of clothing. When everyone in your group is wearing silly clothes, sit down and wait for the others to finish. Ready? Go!**

When all the children are dressed up and seated, have them look at each other. Talk about how the funny clothes make each person look different. For example, you might say, "Taylor looks very dressed up in her fancy dress, but Trevor looks like a cowboy in those boots."

Say: **We can put on silly outfits for fun, but it reminds us that God made us each special on the inside. No two people** are the same—each one is special. There's no one like you! God made you just the way he wanted you to be. Read aloud Psalm 139:14. **God sure is creative to have made each person so different!**

Play the game again, and see how different each person looks. For another variation, let each group have two minutes to dress up one person in the group, making that person look as silly as possible.

Preschool ◐
PLAY POINTER

This is a great opportunity to take a fun and memorable group photo! The next time your group meets, bring enough copies of the photo so everyone can take one home.

Zoo-B-Doo

GROWING CLOSER: God made many different kinds of animals.

KEY VERSE: "For by him all things were created...all things were created by him and for him" (Colossians 1:16).

SUPPLIES: a Bible, animal cookies (You'll need enough cookies so each child can have at least one.)

The Game:

Say: **God made all different kinds of animals for us to enjoy. Let's play a game about God's different animals. Each one of you will get a turn choosing an animal cookie. When you choose a cookie, tell us what animal it is, and we'll act out that animal. Then you can eat your cookie. I'm hungry as a horse...so let's get started!**

Preschool ◐
PLAY POINTER

This is a fun opportunity for you to surprise the children and ham it up! The more dramatic and expressive you are, the easier it will be for children to flex their creative muscles in dramatic play.

Begin the game, giving each child a turn to choose a cookie and tell what animal it is. Allow time for everyone to act out each animal's noises and actions. It's OK if some children pick an animal that has already been acted out. Simply allow children to act out that animal again. When everyone has had a turn, ask:

• **What are some other animals that God created?**

• **What strange things do animals do?**

Say: **God is so creative that he gave the elephant a long trunk, instead of a little nose like ours. God made bugs** that can eat through wood. God even created animals that can fly!

• What things did God make that are not animals?

Say: **The Bible tells us that everything was made by God.** Read aloud the key verse from Colossians 1:16. **God created everything that we see. Even when you see people building a house, you can remember that God made the wood, the sand that makes bricks, the material that makes glass windows...even the metal nails come from rocks that God created! God is creative. He wants us to enjoy all the great things he made.**

You may want to provide extra animal cookies for a snack to celebrate God's creativity.

Sweet Creations

GROWING CLOSER: God created us to be different.

KEY VERSE: "God saw all that he had made, and it was very good" (Genesis 1:31a).

SUPPLIES: a paper lunch sack and candies with distinctive flavors, such as Starburst jelly beans, M&M's (plain and peanut), lemon drops, peppermints, or licorice drops

The Game:

Before children arrive, place a mixture of candies in a paper lunch sack.

Gather children in a circle, and say: **Go around the circle and take turns saying one thing about yourself. You might tell us your name, your favorite food, your birthday, or something about your family.** Begin the game by sharing something about yourself, and then lead children in doing the same. When everyone has shared, ask:

• **What are some ways that the children in this room are the same?**

• **What are some ways that the children in this room are different?**

Say: **God is creative. He made each person here a little different from the next one. God has the best imagination of anyone we know! Even though he created each person**

to be special, God loves us all the same. Let me show you what I mean.

Have children close their eyes while you select a candy from the bag. Eat the candy, then let children open their eyes. Without using the name of the candy, tell children about the candy you ate. Explain what it tasted like. Was it hot? fruity? minty? chocolate? Was the outside of the candy colorful? clear? bright? Did you have to chew it, or did it melt in your mouth? Then let children take turns eating candy and describing the taste to others. When everyone has had a turn, put the candy away. Ask:

• **What was the same about the candy?**

• **What was different about the candy?**

Say: **Even though all the candy was different, it was all sweet and good. God is creative—he made us the same way. We're all different, but each of us is sweet and good to God. In fact, the Bible says that when God saw all the things he had made—and that includes people—he said that they were all good. I'm glad that God is creative and made us all different. Let's enjoy another sweet treat to remember our creative God.**

Let children pass around the bag and play the game again until the candy is all gone.

Preschool PLAY POINTER

Some preschoolers are just developing their vocabulary of adjectives, so you may need to encourage them to think of new descriptive words. This is an excellent (and tasty) activity to help children explain a variety of tastes.

The Seven-Day Game

GROWING CLOSER: God made the world.

KEY VERSE: "This is the account of the heavens and the earth when they were created" (Genesis 2:4a).

SUPPLIES: photocopies of the "Days of Creation" handout (p. 24), scissors, bowl, markers or crayons (optional)

The Game:

Before children arrive, photocopy and cut apart the squares on the "Days of Creation" handout (p. 24). You'll need at least one square for each child. You may want to color the squares to make them more attractive. Place the paper squares in a bowl.

Gather children in a circle, then say: **The Bible tells us that God created the entire world in just six days!**

Ask: • **What things in creation are you most thankful for?**
• **What would it be like if God hadn't created those things?**

Say: **God is creative! Let's act out some of the things God made.** Hold up the bowl and continue: **In this bowl are clues about each day of Creation. Each person will get a card, then I'll tell you what God made on each day. If your card has a picture clue about what God created, stand up and act it out. For example, if I said, "God created the heavens," and you have a picture of the sky, you might stand up and puff out your cheeks like a cloud. Keep acting out your part of Creation until I tell you to stop. Ready?**

Preschool ⬤
PLAY POINTER

Be sure to encourage children, no matter what unique motions they come up with. Applaud their creativity as they invent new and imaginative actions.

Distribute the cards so each child has at least one card. Depending on the number of children in your class, some children may have two cards. Then say: **On the first day, God created light.** Pause and wait for children to act out "light." Let them continue their actions while you continue: **On the second day, God created the heavens.** Pause. **On the third day, God created dry land.** Pause. **On the fourth day, God created the sun.** Pause. **On the fifth day, God created sea creatures and birds.** Pause. **On the sixth day, God created animals and people.** Pause.

Say: **On the seventh day, God rested. You can go ahead and rest, too.** Allow children to sit down. Ask:

• **How do you think God thought up all those neat things?**

Say: **God is so creative—he thought up everything from zebras to tall trees to dandelions! Let's take a moment to thank God for his creation.**

Go around the circle, and let children silently act out one thing that they're glad God created.

Days of Creation

GOD IS
Everywhere

"If I go up to the heavens,

you are there;

if I make my bed in the depths,

you are there."

(Psalm 139:8)

Rollin' Around the World

GROWING CLOSER: God loves people around the world.

KEY VERSE: "After this I looked and there before me was a great multitude that no one could count, from every nation, tribe, people and language, standing before the throne and in front of the Lamb" (Revelation 7:9a).

SUPPLIES: a Bible, masking tape, ball, globe (Optional: Bring in pictures of children from other countries, dressed in native or traditional clothes.)

The Game:

Before the game, make a large masking tape circle on the floor. If you have more than ten children, you may want to make two circles and provide a ball for each group.

Have children sit on the masking tape line with their legs crossed. Hold up the globe and say: **Look at this globe. It is a model of our world and shows all of the places in the world. There are people who live in each part of the land that we see. Those people might look different from us. They might even speak differently from us.**

Set down the globe, and pick up the ball. **Let's pretend that this ball is the world. We'll roll the ball around the circle. Remember to keep the ball on the floor as you roll it to a friend across the circle. As we roll the ball back and forth, let's sing "Jesus Loves the Little Children" to remember all the children around the world.**

As children play, be sure that every child has a turn to roll the ball. After singing the song at least twice, hold the ball and ask:

- **How many people are in the world?**
- **Which people does God love?**

Say: **God isn't just here in this room—God is everywhere! He loves people who live near us and people who live far away from us. There's a verse in the Bible that tells about**

Preschool ◗ PLAY POINTER

Younger preschoolers won't understand the concept of the earth. To cement the idea of many different people, bring in magazine photos of children from different cultures. Point out that God loves everyone, no matter what we look like or how we dress.

lots of people gathering to praise God. Read aloud Revelation 7:9. **This verse tells us that people who worship God look differently, speak differently, and live in different places. But God knows and understands all of them. God is everywhere and loves people from all over.**

Modeling-Dough Planets

GROWING CLOSER: God is bigger than we can imagine.

KEY VERSE: "But will God really dwell on earth with men? The heavens, even the highest heavens, cannot contain you. How much less this temple I have built!" (2 Chronicles 6:18).

SUPPLIES: a variety of colors of modeling dough

The Game:

Give each child a handful of modeling dough. Ask:
- **Where do you think God lives?**
- **What do you think God's house might look like?**

Say: **Even though we don't know what it looks like where God lives, we can imagine what it's like. Use your modeling dough to make a pretend house for God.** Allow children about two or three minutes to create their houses. Then let each person tell about his or her house and why it is a special house for God.

Then say: **The Bible tells us that God doesn't live on earth, as we do. God is so big, that even the sky—outer space— is too big for him! Instead of building houses for God, let's use our modeling dough to make planets. The planets can remind us that God is even too big for outer space!**

Give each child another small handful of a different color of modeling dough. Show children how to marble the colors together and roll the dough into a "planet" or ball. When each child has a planet, ask:

Preschool
PLAY POINTER

If time allows, have children form pairs and sit at a table, across from their partners. Let partners roll their "planets" back and forth. Each time children roll their planets, have them tell one place God is. Children might say, "God is in the mountains," "God is in the clouds," or "God is in my kitchen."

• If God is so big, how can he listen to us?

• If God is bigger than outer space, how does he watch what we're doing?

Say: **God *is* greater than the heavens, but he also can fit right into our hearts! That's because God is everywhere. God is bigger than the sky, and small enough to sit with you in your bedroom. God is more gigantic than the tallest building, but he's just the right size to hold us when we feel sad. Use your dough to make a heart.** Allow a minute or two for children to shape their dough into heart shapes.

Say: **Take these modeling-dough hearts home as a reminder that even though God is big and mighty, he can live in our hearts.**

Guess Who's Talking

GROWING CLOSER: God is everywhere.

KEY VERSE: "The priests and the Levites stood to bless the people, and God heard them, for their prayer reached heaven, his holy dwelling place" (2 Chronicles 30:27).

SUPPLIES: a Bible, an audiocassette recorder and a blank cassette tape

The Game:

Before children arrive, practice with the cassette recorder and blank tape to be sure it will pick up a speaking voice and replay it clearly.

Gather the children in an area where the tape recorder can be easily used. Demonstrate how the machine works by recording yourself on the tape and replaying it for the children. Say: **Each of us is going to record a message on the tape. Then we'll play the tape and see if we can guess who is talking. I will push the buttons on the tape recorder as each of you takes a turn saying "God knows my voice when I talk to him." Let's say that together.** Lead children in saying the sentence.

Go around the group, and let children take turns speaking into the recorder. (You may want to jot down the order in which children speak.) Be sure to leave a brief space after each voice so you'll be able to stop and start the tape without cutting off anyone's words.

When everyone has had a turn, rewind the tape to the beginning. Have children find a new place in the circle to make the game more challenging. Say: **Now we will listen to the tape and see if we can guess who is speaking.** Play the tape and see if children can recognize each other's voices or even their own voices. The children may be surprised to hear the voice identified as their own, because it might sound different from the way they hear themselves. Ask:

Preschool
PLAY POINTER
Be aware that some children may be shy about speaking into a recorder. Allow them to observe several others first, then try it if they wish.

• **What do you think it's like for God to hear all of our different voices?**

Say: **The Bible tells us what happened when God's people prayed and talked to him.** Read aloud 2 Chronicles 30:27 from an easy-to-understand Bible translation. Continue: **God knows the voice of each person who talks to him. But God doesn't just hear our voices—God watches all that we do. He knows how we speak and how we act and how we think. That's because God is everywhere. God doesn't just have to guess by the sound of our voices. He is with us and knows all that we do.**

Always Watching

GROWING CLOSER: God watches over us, whatever we're doing.

KEY VERSE: "The Lord watches over you—the Lord is your shade at your right hand" (Psalm 121:5).

SUPPLIES: a Bible, paper towel or toilet paper tubes (or construction paper), crayons

The Game:

Distribute cardboard tubes so each child has one. (If you have a large class, tape sheets of construction paper into tubes.) Set out crayons, and allow children to decorate their tubes.

Say: **Let's pretend that these tubes are telescopes. Hold your telescope up to your eye and look around the room.** Allow children to experiment with their telescopes for a few seconds. **Now let's play a game of I Spy. I'll look around the** room with my telescope until I see—or "spy"—something interesting. Then I'll say, "I spy, with my little eye, something that..." and I'll tell you what I see. Then you can look for it with your telescopes.

Look around the circle, and fix your telescope on a child. Say: **I spy, with my little eye, someone God loves very much.** Pause while other children look at the child through their telescopes. Then continue: **I spy, with my little eye, someone that God watches over all the time.** Continue the game, affirming children and reminding them of God's love and care for them.

When every child has been affirmed, say: **Just as I watched all of you with my telescope, God watches over everyone.** Read aloud Psalm 121:5. **God sees everything that you do, no matter where you go. Let's sing a song to remember that God is always watching over us.**

Lead children in the following song, to the tune of "Jesus Loves Me."

Preschool
PLAY POINTER
This is a great way to review past lessons, Bible verses, or help children get to know one another's names.

> **God is watching over you** (point to any child),
> **He can see all that you do.** (Look through telescope.)
> **In the day or when it's night** (stretch, then lay head on hands),
> **You are always in his sight.** (Look through telescope.)
> **God always sees us,**
> **God always sees us,**
> **God always sees us,**
> **He's always watching you!** (Point to any child.)

Let children take their telescopes home as reminders that God is always watching them, no matter where they go.

Hide and See

GROWING CLOSER: God sees everything.

KEY VERSE: " 'Can anyone hide in secret places so that I cannot see him?' declares the Lord. 'Do not I fill heaven and earth?' declares the Lord" (Jeremiah 23:24).

SUPPLIES: paper, crayons

The Game:

Say: **We're going to start out by playing a quick game of Hide-and-Seek. You'll hide, and I'll try to find you. Ready? Go!** Keep your eyes open, and watch where children hide. Then walk around the room, find them, and bring them back to the middle of the room.

When you've gathered all the children, ask:

- **Why was it so easy for me to find you?**

- **When people usually play Hide-and-Seek, what makes it harder to find people?**

Say: **I kept my eyes open so I would know where you went. God keeps his eyes on us all the time. There's no place we can go where God can't see us! We can't hide from God, and we can't hide our actions from God, either. To see what that's like, let's draw some pictures.**

Distribute crayons and paper, and instruct children to scatter around the room so no one will be able to see their drawings. Allow them to draw whatever they wish for one minute. Then have children gather in a circle, holding their pictures face down.

Say: **Now I'll try to guess what each person has drawn.** Go around the circle and make silly guesses as to what children might have drawn. After each guess, have that child hold up his or her picture and tell what it's a picture of. When you've guessed each picture, ask:

- **How did I do at guessing?**
- **Why were my guesses so wrong?**

Say: **I couldn't see what you drew, but God never has to guess. He could see every picture that each person drew. God is everywhere—we can't hide from God.**

Preschool ●
PLAY POINTER

If your room doesn't allow many (if any) places to hide, take children outside and specify the area in which they may hide.

Sticking With God

GROWING CLOSER: God never leaves us.
KEY VERSE: "And God said, 'I will be with you'" (Exodus 3:12a).
SUPPLIES: a Bible, a variety of stickers

The Game:

Read aloud Exodus 3:12a, then give each child at least one sheet of stickers. Say: **We'll use these stickers to see what it's like to know that God is always with us. I'll call out a place or time that God is with you. I might say, "God is with you at home" or "God is with you in the car." You'll find someone and put a sticker on him or her, then tell that person, "God always sticks with you!" Then you'll sit down until I call out something new. Try to put your stickers on a different person each time. Keep your stickers on until the end of the game. Ready?**

Call out the following places: at home, in the car, at the park, at church, at school, in the bathtub, when I'm on vacation, in a storm, when I watch TV, and in the dark. When children are covered with stickers, ask:

• **How does it make you feel to know that God is always with you?**

• **How can God be with everyone all the time?**

Say: **God is so big that he can stick with every person, all the time. Let's close with a special prayer, thanking God for being with us everywhere we go.**

Lead children in this simple prayer.

God, you're with me in the dark,
In a storm, at the park.
There is no place I can go
Where you'll leave me all alone.
I'm so glad, God, that you care
And that you're with me everywhere! Amen.

GOD IS
Faithful

"Know therefore
that the Lord your God is God;
he is the faithful God,
keeping his covenant of love
to a thousand generations
of those who love him
and keep his commands."
(Deuteronomy 7:9)

A Clothespin Buddy

GROWING CLOSER: We can be brave, because God is with us.

KEY VERSE: "God has said, 'Never will I leave you; never will I forsake you.' " So we say with confidence, 'The Lord is my helper; I will not be afraid.' " (Hebrews 13:5b-6a).

SUPPLIES: a Bible, clothespins, small squares of paper (You may want to use a permanent marker to write, "God Never Leaves Us" on each clothespin.)

The Game:

Ask: • **How do you feel when you're alone?**

• **Who would you like to have with you when you're afraid?**

Say: **Sometimes we feel afraid or alone. This game will help us learn about someone who is always with us.**

Give each child a square of paper, and instruct children to place the papers on their shoulders. Say: **Now, see if you can shake the paper off your shoulder, without using your hands.** When children have tried this, say: **That was too easy. Let's make this game a little more challenging!**

Clip a clothespin to each child's back, close enough to children's shoulders so they can feel and see it, but not where it can be easily reached. When every child is "wearing" a clothespin, say: **Now, try to shake these clothespins off, without using your hands.** Allow children to jump, hop, shake, and move about as they try to loosen the clothespins. (They'll have a great time trying!) After a minute, gather children and ask:

• **Which was easier to lose, the paper or the clothespin? Why?**

Say: **The Bible teaches us that God is faithful—he never leaves us. God never walks away. God isn't like the piece of paper—something that easily falls away. Instead, God is more like the clothespin. God stays with us wherever we go.** Ask:

• **How do you feel, knowing that God will never leave you?**

• **When might be a good time to remember that God is with you?**

Preschool ⬤
PLAY POINTER

If you have older preschoolers, you may want to ask how they knew that the clothespins were on their backs. Help children understand that, even though we can't *see* God, we can trust that he's always there.

Read aloud Hebrews 13:5b-6a from an easy-to-understand Bible translation. Say: **Because God is with us, we don't have to be afraid. We can be brave because we're never alone!**

Let children wear their clothespins home as a reminder that God never leaves us.

Follow the Plan

GROWING CLOSER: God is faithful.

KEY VERSE: " 'For I know the plans I have for you,' declares the Lord, 'plans to prosper you and not to harm you, plans to give you hope and a future' " (Jeremiah 29:11).

SUPPLIES: envelopes, masking tape, scissors, 11X17-inch construction paper, markers

The Game:

Before the game, draw a large heart on a sheet of construction paper, then color in the heart. Cut the heart picture into several large pieces (at least ten) and place each piece in a separate envelope. Tape half of the envelopes in obvious places, such as on the wall, on top of tables, or on windows. Tape the rest of the envelopes in less obvious places, such as in cabinet doors or under chair seats.

Gather children and say: **There are special envelopes hidden around the room. Each envelope has part of a message inside. We're going to hunt for all the envelopes to find out what the message is. First, let's make a plan to help us find all the envelopes.** Ask:

• **What are some ways we can get to the envelopes?** Children might mention things such as walking, running, hopping, crawling, or tiptoeing.

Say: **Some of the envelopes will be easy to find—you can probably see them right now! But other envelopes will be harder to find. You'll need to follow my plan to find them all so we can hear the special message.**

Preschool
PLAY POINTER

As they arrive, children may point out some of the more visible envelopes. If so, just explain that the envelopes are for a game and must stay put for now, so everyone can play the game together.

Lead children around the room, traveling in the different ways that children mentioned. You might also have children count their steps, walk around furniture, jump over low obstacles, crawl under a table, move like animals, or walk sideways. Allow a different child to retrieve each envelope and hand it to you.

After all the envelopes have been found, let children work together to tape the pieces together to form the heart. When the picture is finished, ask:

- **What is God's message to us?**
- **How does God show his love to you?**
- **How do you show your love to God?**

Say: **The Bible tells us that God loves us and has good plans for us.** Ask:

- **What would have happened if you didn't follow my plans in the game?**

Say: **If you hadn't followed my plans, you wouldn't have found all the envelopes. If we don't follow God's good plans, we'll miss out on all the great things he may have for us. God is faithful—we can trust that God's plans are good!**

You may want to allow children to make their own heart puzzles to take home. Children can lead their families through the "message search," too!

Catch Me!

GROWING CLOSER: God never turns away from us.

KEY VERSE: "And God is faithful; he will not let you be tempted beyond what you can bear. But when you are tempted, he will also provide a way out so that you can stand up under it" (1 Corinthians 10:13b).

SUPPLIES: none

The Game:

Gather children and have them stand in a tight circle. It's important that children stand shoulder to shoulder.

Say: **We're going to play a trusting game. I need one person to stand in**

Preschool
PLAY POINTER

Keep your circle tight and small, so the person in the middle can't really lean too far. This makes it easier for others to catch him or her, and makes the experience less threatening so more children will want to try.

the middle of our circle. **That person will slowly fall forward or backward, and we'll catch him or her. When you catch someone, gently push the person back toward the middle of the circle.** Choose a volunteer and have the child stand in the center of the circle with arms at his or her side and feet together. Encourage the child to slowly sway backward or forward, and guide others in catching the child.

After about thirty seconds, let another child be in the middle. Let several children try the "center" role—as many as your time allows. Then have children sit down. Ask:

• **What was it like to be in the middle of the circle?**

• **What would have happened if we all turned away from the person in the middle?**

Say: **The Bible tells us that God never turns away from us. When we're afraid or scared or sad, God will help us. Just as the person in this game could lean on us, we can lean on God. He will always catch us and help us.**

Lead children in singing this song, to the tune of "Frère Jacques," as a reminder of God's faithfulness.

God is faithful.
God is faithful.
All the time.
All the time.
God won't let us fall—
Not one bit at all!
We can trust.
We can trust.

Preschool ◗
PLAY POINTER

If any children fall or aren't caught in the game, point out that people sometimes let us down, but God is 100 percent faithful. Explain that we can always trust that God will be there when we need him—even when people aren't!

Shadow Dance

GROWING CLOSER: God never leaves us.
KEY VERSE: "See, I have engraved you on the palms of my hands" (Isaiah 49:16a).
SUPPLIES: an overhead projector

The Game:

Before the game, set up an overhead projector so that it shines the light against the wall at floor level. Back up the projector so there is a large lit area on the wall.

Say: **Look at the palms of your hands. That's the side without any fingernails!** Ask:

• **What do you see on the palms of your hands?**

• **Do you think you could scrub away those tiny lines? Why or why not?**

Say: **Those little lines on your hands are just part of the way God made you. They'll be there forever! In the Bible, God says that he "engraved" us on the palms of his hands. That's sort of like these tiny lines on our hands—they're always with us, and we're always with God. That's because God is faithful. Let's play a game to learn more about God's faithfulness.**

Have children stand in front of the light, facing their own shadows on the wall. Say: **We're going to play a game with our shadows. You need to listen for my instructions and do what I say. OK?**

Lead children through the following actions:

Take one step toward the wall.
Take one step back.
Touch your head.
Touch your toes.
Wiggle your hands.
Run in place.
Wave your hands in the air.
Touch your knees.
Touch your shoulders.
Turn around.
Sit down.

Ask: • **What did your shadow do during that game?**

• **Could you have done anything to make your shadow do a different action than you were doing?**

Preschool
PLAY POINTER

If it's sunny outside and the conditions are "shadow-friendly," you may want to take children outside for this activity. Play Follow the Leader's Shadow and let them see their shadows fall on concrete, sand, flowers, grass, walls, or other interesting surfaces. You may even connect the various surfaces to the fact that God is with us in any situation.

Say: **The Bible tells us that God will never leave us, sort of like the way your shadow wouldn't leave you.** Ask:
• **Why do you think God is always with you?**
• **How does it make you feel to know that God will never leave you?**
Say: **Just like our shadows in this game, God will never leave us. He's always nearby, faithfully watching over us. Whenever you see your shadow, you can remember that God is right beside you.**

Treasure Maps

GROWING CLOSER: God has a plan for us.
KEY VERSE: "All the days planned for me were written in your book before I was one day old" (Psalm 139:16b, New Century Version).
SUPPLIES: a Bible, markers or crayons, paper, a plate of treats

The Game:

Before children arrive, hide a plate of treats somewhere in the room.

Gather children and say: **I've hidden a plate of goodies somewhere in this room. Let's see if anyone can figure out where they might be hidden. Instead of telling me, you will use the paper and markers to draw a map that you think will lead to the treats. Be sure to draw things that are in our room, to help everyone understand where the treats might be hidden.**

Distribute the paper and markers, then give children a minute or two to draw simple "treasure maps" that will lead to the treats. Then let children show their maps and explain where they think the goodies are hidden. Follow as many maps as possible, until you find the treats. While children are enjoying their snacks, ask:
• **What else do we use maps for?**
• **What would happen if we didn't have maps?**

Preschool PLAY POINTER

Since preschoolers are still fine-tuning their drawing skills, it's likely that their treasure maps won't be clear to anyone except the artist. Simply allow children to explain where their maps lead, or let each child lead the group on a unique treasure hunt.

Say: **The Bible tells us that God has planned out our lives—it's as if God has a map of where your life will lead.** Read aloud Psalm 139:16b from an easy-to-understand Bible translation. **Sometimes we may feel lost, but God has good things planned for us—just as I had good treats tucked away in this room! We can trust that God is faithful and will guide us each day of our lives. With God, we're never lost.**

Peter's Trust Walk

GROWING CLOSER: We can trust God.
KEY VERSE: "Immediately Jesus reached out his hand and caught him. 'You of little faith,' he said, 'why did you doubt?' " (Matthew 14:31).
SUPPLIES: a large sheet

The Game:

Spread out the sheet, and have children sit around the edges. Say: **I'm going to tell you a story, and we'll use this sheet to help act out the story. Are you ready?**

This story begins when Jesus had a busy day. He had been talking and telling people about God. All that talking and teaching made Jesus tired! So Jesus told his friends to get into a boat and sail across the lake, while he went to rest and pray. Let's pretend this sheet is the lake that Jesus' friends were sailing on. Lead children in kneeling and "rowing" across the "lake." Let children row across the lake and find a new place to sit at the edge of the sheet.

Continue: **Jesus' friends had been out on the boat for a while, when the wind started blowing, making big, splashy** waves. **Let's make waves with our sheet.** Lead children in wiggling the edges of the sheet to create "waves." **Suddenly, someone looked out of the boat and saw something... something that looked like a ghost! They were scared! Use the sheet to cover your eyes, as if you were afraid.** Lead children in holding the edge of the sheet up to their eyes.

Say: **But it wasn't a ghost—it was Jesus! He was walking on the water! You can take the sheet away from your eyes now. Jesus said, "It is I. Don't be afraid." One of Jesus' friends, Peter, called out, "Lord, if it's you, tell me to come to you on the water." So Jesus called Peter to come...and Peter stepped out of the boat and began walking on top of the water! Let's step on our sheet and pretend that we're Peter.** Lead children in gently walking across the sheet, as if it's water. Then have children sit down. Ask:

• **Why do you think Peter wanted to walk to Jesus?**
• **What would you have done if you were in the boat?**

Continue: **Peter took several steps toward Jesus, but then he noticed something. The wind and the waves splashed at his feet.** Lead children in making waves again. **Peter was afraid that he would sink into the water! Let's put our feet under the water to show how Peter's feet were sinking.** When children's feet are covered, ask:

• **What would you do if you were Peter?**

Continue: **Peter called out, "Lord, save me!" Immediately, Jesus reached out and caught Peter. They both climbed into the boat, where they were safe. As soon as Jesus and Peter were in the boat, something amazing happened. The wind stopped and the water got very still. Let's smooth out our sheet to show how calm and still the water might have been.** Lead children in pulling the sheet taut so it's smooth. Ask:

• **Why did Jesus help Peter?**
• **How does God help you?**
• **Why do you think God helps you?**

Say: **God is faithful. Just as Peter trusted Jesus enough to walk on the water, we can trust God when we have to do hard things. God loves us and will help us, just as Jesus helped Peter. Let's huddle under our sheet for a quick prayer. We'll thank God for being so faithful to us.**

Lead children in lifting the sheet overhead, ducking underneath, then sitting on the edge of the sheet in a "sheet bubble." Pray: **God, thank you that you are faithful and that we can trust in you. Thank you for helping us do hard things. Amen.**

Preschool
PLAY POINTER

You may want to let children take turns walking across the sheet "lake" while others sit around the edges and make waves. (The wavemakers can make storm noises for an even greater effect!)

GOD IS
Forgiving

"Who is a God like you,

who pardons sin

and forgives the transgression

of the remnant of his inheritance?

You do not stay angry forever

but delight to show mercy."

(Micah 7:18)

The Biggest Hug

GROWING CLOSER: God's forgiveness brings us close to him.

KEY VERSE: "Come near to God and he will come near to you" (James 4:8a).

SUPPLIES: a Bible (If you have younger preschoolers, you may want to use masking tape to make a circle on the floor to help them walk in a circle.)

The Game:

Ask: • **What happens when you do something wrong?**
• **Do others still love you when you do something wrong? How can you tell?**

Say: **We sometimes do wrong or bad things. Those are called sins, and our sins make God sad. But even when we sin, God forgives us and shows us his love. When God forgives us, we can be close to him again! There's a verse in the Bible that tells us about feeling close to God.** Read aloud James 4:8a from an easy-to-understand Bible translation. Then say: **Let's play a game to learn more about that special verse.**

In this game, we'll walk around in a circle while I say our special Bible verse. When you hear me say the last word of the verse, stop where you are and find someone to hug. Then we'll say the verse together. Are you ready?

Join children in walking in a circle, then say: **"Come near to God and he will come near to you."** Find a child to hug, then lead children in saying the verse together. Repeat the game, speeding up and slowing down the tempo of your speech, so children won't know until the last second when they should stop walking.

Then gather children in a circle and say: **We can't hug God like we hug each other, because God doesn't have a body like ours. But we can feel close to God in other ways.** Ask:

• **What are some ways you can be close to God?** Children may respond that they can pray, sing songs about God, or listen to Bible stories.

Preschool ● PLAY POINTER

Although you want to focus on God's forgiveness, you can also bring in the idea of showing forgiveness to others. Ask children, "When is it hard to forgive others?" or "How is forgiveness like a big hug?" Help children understand that when we forgive, we are showing others God's forgiveness, too.

• **What does it feel like to feel close to God?**
Join together for a group hug and say the verse together.

Forgiveness Dance

GROWING CLOSER: God forgives everyone.
KEY VERSE: "You are forgiving and good, O Lord, abounding in love to all who call to you" (Psalm 86:5).
SUPPLIES: a Bible

The Game:

Show children the American Sign Language sign for "forgive." Brush your right palm with your left palm, then brush your left palm with your right. Say: **This sign is easy to remember, because you can pretend you got some dirt on your hands, and you're wiping it off. God's forgiveness is sort of like that, because God wipes away the bad things we do.** Read aloud Psalm 86:5. Then continue: **Let's celebrate God's forgiveness with this song and dance.**

Form a circle, then teach children this song to the tune of "Frère Jacques."

Preschool
PLAY POINTER
You may want to begin this activity by playing outside in a sandbox or other "dirty" area. Bring children inside and distribute baby wipes. Allow children to use the wipes to clean their hands and see all the dirt that comes off.

God forgives us (sign for "forgive"),
God forgives us (sign for "forgive"),
Every one (put arms on neighbors' shoulders and step right),
Every one. (Leave arms on neighbors' shoulders and step right again.)
God forgives you (point to someone),
God forgives me (point to yourself),
Every one (put arms on neighbors' shoulders and step left),
Every one. (Leave arms on neighbors' shoulders and step left again.)

When children are familiar with the song, replace "you" and "me" with children's names. Continue until you've sung everyone's name, including your own. Then say: **The Bible teaches us that**

God forgives everyone who asks, and that he loves everyone who calls on him. That's a good thing to know! God knows our names and loves us.

Close by singing the song and dancing again.

Rock Pile

GROWING CLOSER: God sent Jesus to take away our sins.

KEY VERSE: "If we confess our sins, he is faithful and just and will forgive us our sins and purify us from all unrighteousness" (1 John 1:9).

SUPPLIES: a Bible, one rock and one marshmallow per child, one bowl or basket, one feather (or other soft item), masking tape, cassette player, cassette of upbeat music

The Game:

Before the children arrive, use the masking tape to make a large circle on the floor. Place the marshmallows in a bowl or basket and set it aside.

Have children sit on the masking tape circle. Give each child a rock and say: **Hold your rock in your hands. These are just plain rocks that came from my yard. There's nothing special about them at all. Let's pretend these rocks are sins. Sins are the bad things we say, think, and do. Even though God always loves us, God doesn't like those things. Let's try to get rid of these sins.**

Hold up the feather and say: **When I touch you with this feather, run to a friend and trade rocks with him or her, then go back to your place in the circle. Ready?** Demonstrate how to trade a rock with a child. Then put on some upbeat music and begin the game. After every child has had a turn to trade rocks, ask:

Preschool
PLAY POINTER

Although you don't have to use a feather or soft item to touch children, children will enjoy the novelty and tactile sensation of it. This is a simple way to intrigue and engage children, as well as delight them! You may even want to explain that God's forgiveness is gentle and soft, just like a feather.

• **Did anyone get anything different from a rock?**

Say: **Everyone got to trade rocks, so you each have a different rock. But it's still a rock! You didn't really get rid of it at all! It takes something special to take away our sins, too. Let's see what the Bible tells us.** Read aloud 1 John 1:9 from an easy-to-understand Bible translation. Say: **Let's ask God to forgive us for the bad things we've said, thought, or done.** Lead children in this simple prayer: **Dear God, we all have done wrong things. Please forgive us for our sins. Make us brand new and clean. Amen.**

Set the basket of marshmallows in the center of the circle.

Say: **Now, let's play this game again. This time, when I touch you with the feather, run to the middle of the circle and trade your rock for a tasty marshmallow. These marshmallows will remind us that Jesus forgives our sins and makes our lives wonderful and new. When you get back to your place in the circle, you may eat your tasty marshmallow.**

Play the upbeat music, and begin the game. As children are enjoying their marshmallows, remind children that God is forgiving. Explain that we can celebrate and praise God for his love and forgiveness.

Perfect Love

GROWING CLOSER: God's love and forgiveness is perfect.
KEY VERSE: "For I will forgive their wickedness and will remember their sins no more" (Jeremiah 31:34b).
SUPPLIES: a Bible, transparent tape, construction paper, scissors

The Game:

Before children arrive, stack two sheets of construction paper and cut two identical, large hearts. Set aside one of the hearts.

Hold up the other heart and say: **This heart is pretty and perfect! It doesn't have any wrinkles in it or anything! We'll pretend this is like the heart inside each one of us—the heart that makes us feel happy and sad. If I said something mean to someone** (tear a piece from the heart) **that person's heart would feel sad and broken. Let's pass this heart** around the circle and let each person tear off a piece of the heart. While you do this, think of something you've done or said that made someone feel sad. Pass the heart around, and let children tear pieces off and hold the pieces in their laps.

When the remainder of the heart comes back to you, hold it up and ask:

• **What's left of our heart?**

• **How can we make this heart look nice again?**

Say: **Let's see if we can work together and put all the pieces of the heart back together.** Help children piece together the heart, like a puzzle, and lay it on the floor in the middle of the circle. Then say: **When we've done mean or hurtful things, we need people to forgive us. Forgiveness makes our hearts right again.** Hold up the transparent tape. **Let's pretend this tape is like forgiveness. It will help mend this sad and broken heart.**

Preschool
PLAY POINTER

If you have more than ten children, form pairs and give each pair a heart. Have partners take turns tearing large pieces off the heart as they think of hurtful things. Then allow partners to work together to "mend" the heart.

Give children each a piece of tape, and have them add their piece to help mend the paper heart. As children add their pieces, have them each say, "Please forgive me" or "I forgive you." When the heart is mended, say: **Forgiveness helped make this heart better.** Ask:

• **Does the heart look as nice as it did before? Why or why not?**

Say: **Forgiveness *does* make us feel better, but it can't make our hearts perfect. But the Bible tells us that when God forgives us, his love *is* perfect.** Read aloud Jeremiah 31:34b, then bring out the other "perfect" heart. **This verse says that when God forgives us, he doesn't even remember our sins. It's like God has a perfect heart—our sins are completely gone!**

GOD IS
Giving

"Every good and perfect gift
is from above,
coming down from the Father
of the heavenly lights,
who does not change
like shifting shadows."
(James 1:17)

Family Fame Game

GROWING CLOSER: God gives us families.

KEY VERSE: "I kneel before the Father, from whom his whole family in heaven and on earth derives its name" (Ephesians 3:14b-15).

SUPPLIES: a Bible, Family Fame Game cube (p. 51), scissors, tape

The Game:

Before the game, photocopy the Family Fame Game cube sheet (p. 51), cut it apart, and tape it together to form a cube.

Hold up the game cube and say: **In this game we'll share stories about the people pictured on this cube. When you roll the cube, you get to tell a quick story or something you love about the person on the top of the cube. You can tell a story about someone in your own family, someone in a different family, or someone that you heard about in a story.**

Begin by rolling the cube and telling a quick story about the person on the cube. Then have children take turns rolling the game cube. You may need to help them think of things each family member can do or things that make family members special. Remember to be sensitive to children who may have nontraditional family settings.

After everyone has had a turn to tell a story, ask:

• **Who are some people in your family?**

• **What would it be like if you were the only one in your family?**

• **Why do you think God gave you a family?**

Read aloud Ephesians 3:14b-15. Say: **This verse tells us that all families come from God. Families are important to God, in fact, we all belong to God's family! Every family looks different—some have fathers, some have brothers and sisters, some have grandparents and aunts and uncles. Sometimes neighbors and friends love each other so much that they feel like a family. Families are one of the best gifts God has given us!**

Preschool PLAY POINTER

You may want to photocopy the cube and give one to each child. Let children color the cubes to represent their families. Then they can take the cubes home, roll them, and hug the person whose picture appears on the top side of the cube.

Family Fame Game

Brother

Mother

Grandmother

Sister

Father

Grandfather

Teddy Tumble

GROWING CLOSER: God gives us what we need.

KEY VERSE: "If you, then, though you are evil, know how to give good gifts to your children, how much more will your Father in heaven give good gifts to those who ask him!" (Matthew 7:11).

SUPPLIES: one teddy bear, one laundry basket, enough socks for each child to have one

The Game:

Place the teddy bear in the laundry basket, and set it at one side of the room. Have children line up along the opposite wall of the room. Choose one or two children to be "It," and have them step away from the wall. Give the rest of the children each a sock.

Say: **We're going to play Teddy Tumble. The teddy bear is in the basket, but the basket is hard and uncomfortable. Let's give the teddy bear our socks so that he'll have something soft to tumble in. When I say "Teddy Tumble," you'll all run to the other side of the room and toss your socks in with the teddy bear. You'll need to run fast, because "It" will try to tag you before you get to the teddy! If you get tagged, go back to the starting wall and try again. Ready? Teddy Tumble!**

Let children play several rounds, allowing new people to be "It" each time. Then gather children around the laundry basket.

Ask: • **Why did the teddy bear need our socks?**

• **What things do you need?**

• **Who gives you the things you need?**

Say: **The Bible book of Matthew says that God gives us good things. God loves us so much, that he wouldn't give us something that was bad.** Ask:

• **What are some good things that God has given you?**

Say: **Just as you took care of the teddy bear, God takes care of us. He gives us families who love us, teachers**

Preschool PLAY POINTER

To extend this activity, you may want to set out cotton batting and allow children to stuff the socks you've given them, creating little pillows. Then tie a knot at the open end of each sock and allow children to use markers or fabric crayons to decorate their pillows. Explain that the pillows can remind us that God gently takes care of our needs.

who help us learn, and churches where we can learn even more about him! Let's pray and thank God for his good gifts.

Pray: **Dear God, thank you for all the wonderful things you give us. We're glad that you always give us good things. We love you. Amen.**

The Greatest Gift

GROWING CLOSER: God loves us and sent Jesus.

KEY VERSE: "For God so loved the world that he gave his one and only Son, that whoever believes in him shall not perish but have eternal life" (John 3:16).

SUPPLIES: a Bible, small bean bag, Hershey's Kisses candies or candy hearts

The Game:

Have the children sit in a circle. Hold up the bean bag and say: **In this game, we'll toss this bean bag to each other. When you catch the bean bag, finish this sentence, "I show someone love, when I..." You might say that you show someone love by bringing them a drink, helping them clean up, feeding the cat, or saying nice words to them. Ready?**

Begin the game by completing the sentence, "I show someone love when I..." then gently toss the bean bag to a child. You may need to offer ideas or encourage children to help each other think of ways to show love. When everyone has had a turn, hold the bean bag and ask:

• **How do you feel when you show someone love?**

• **What are some ways that people show they love you?**

• **How do you feel when someone shows love to you?**

Say: **The Bible tells us that God loved us so much that he gave us Jesus.** Read aloud John 3:16, then continue: **God loves us and sent Jesus. Just as we show others how much we love them, God showed his love by sending Jesus. Because God sent Jesus to love and teach us, we can live with God forever! Jesus is the greatest gift!**

Preschool
PLAY POINTER

You may want to place the Hershey's Kisses candies or candy hearts in a gift bag or wrap them in gift wrap. Talk about how special it feels to receive a good gift.

Give each child two Hershey's Kisses candies or candy hearts. Explain that one treat is to keep and one is to give to someone they love.

Fishing for Animals

GROWING CLOSER: God gave us a beautiful world.
KEY VERSE: "God blessed them and said to them, '...Rule over the fish of the sea and the birds of the air and over every living creature that moves on the ground'" (Genesis 1:28).
SUPPLIES: a Bible, pictures of animals from magazines or coloring books, scissors, tape, paper clips, one yard of string, one magnet, a yardstick or other sturdy pole

The Game:

Before children arrive, cut the animal pictures in half, and tape a paper clip to the back of each half. You will need one-half of an animal picture for every child. (If there is an uneven number of children, play the game with them.) Tie or tape the magnet to the string, and then tie the string to the yardstick or pole.

Have children form a circle of chairs, facing the middle of the circle. This is your "pond."

Say: **Let's pretend this circle is a pond. One fun thing to do at a pond is to go fishing.** Ask:
• **Have you ever been fishing? What was it like?**
• **Why do people like to catch fish?**

Say: **Fishing is one way to catch animals. Let's use this fishing pole to see what animals we can catch.**

Drop all the animal pictures in the middle of the pond. Hang the fishing line into the pond to demonstrate how to "fish." Touch the magnet to the paper clip, and pull in your "catch." (If any pictures stick together, take one and drop the rest back into the pond.) Hold up the picture, and ask children to identify the animal. If children can't identify the animal, have them wait until the matching half is caught. Let each child have a turn to fish for animals. Have children

Preschool ●
PLAY POINTER

Preschoolers love making animal noises! As children figure out what animals they've "caught," you may allow them to make the noise the animal makes or imitate the animal. Children will love roaring, hopping, chirping, and galloping!

pair up with the person who catches the other half of their animal. When all the animals have been caught, instruct partners to sit facing each other, placing their animal pictures in front of them. Let partners tell what animal they caught, then ask:

• **Why do you think God gave us animals?**
• **What would the world be like without animals?**

Say: **God is giving. The Bible tells us that God gave people all the animals on earth, in the water, and in the air.** Read aloud Genesis 1:28. **God gave us animals as a way of taking care of us. God's animals give us meat to eat, wool to keep us warm, milk to drink, and lots of other good things.** Lead children in a group prayer. Go around the circle and let each child say, "Thank you, God, for giving us [name of the animal in front of them]."

Ravens to the Rescue

GROWING CLOSER: God takes care of our needs.
KEY VERSE: "You will drink from the brook, and I have ordered the ravens to feed you there" (1 Kings 17:4).
SUPPLIES: a box of small crackers or cookies, plastic sandwich bags or plastic wrap

The Game:

Before the game, prepare a snack for each child by putting several cookies or crackers into a plastic sandwich bag or wrapped in a sheet of plastic wrap. Set the packages on a table that is easy for children to reach.

Have children form a circle. Say: **God is giving. He knows what we need and will always take good care of us. In the Bible, a man named Elijah was hungry, so God sent ravens—big black birds—to feed Elijah. We're going to get our snack today by taking turns being ravens.** Choose a child to be the first raven.

Lead children in the following rhyme:

Elijah was hungry and he rested his head. *(Children lean forward, put their heads down, and close their eyes.)*
God sent the ravens to give him some bread. *(The*

raven "flies" to the snack area and picks up one of the packages.)

Fly away, fly away, raven fly high! (The raven flies around the circle.)

Fly away, raven, to feed that guy! (Raven flies to any child and quietly puts the snack behind him or her. Then the raven flies back to his or her place in the circle.)

Elijah, Elijah, something is new!

See how God is caring for you. (Children sit up and look to see who received the snack.)

The child chosen as "Elijah" leaves the snack at his or her place and becomes the raven. As the game progresses, the raven can tell who has already been served by seeing who has a snack behind him or her. Repeat the rhyming game until everyone has been served.

Say: **God cares for us, just as he cared for Elijah when Elijah was hungry. Let's thank God for our snack and for taking good care of us.** Lead children in a simple prayer.

GOD IS
King

"Sing praises to God,

sing praises;

sing praises to our King,

sing praises.

For God is the King of all the earth;

sing to him a psalm of praise."

(Psalm 47:6-7)

I Spy, God on High

GROWING CLOSER: God is worthy of our praise.

KEY VERSE: "Great is the Lord and most worthy of praise; his greatness no one can fathom" (Psalm 145:3).

SUPPLIES: a Bible

The Game:

Say: **God is our king. Even though we don't have many real kings today, maybe you've heard of a king in a storybook.** Ask:

- **How do people treat a king?**
- **What do people say to kings?**

Say: **Let's see what the Bible says about God, our King.** Read aloud Psalm 145:3 from an easy-to-understand Bible translation. Continue: **This verse says that God is great—so great that we can praise and thank him. Let's play a game that helps us name things we can praise God for. I'll start by saying, "I spy something red."** Look around the room for something red. **If you think you know what I'm praising God for, jump up and say, "You're praising God for..."** then name the object. Got it?

Begin the I Spy game by choosing something clearly visible in the room, such as a plant, a pitcher of water, a Bible, or food. Then let another child have a turn. After several children have had turns, ask:

- **What other things can we thank God for?**
- **How can we show God we're thankful and happy for all he's given us?**

Say: **God has put many things in our lives that make us happy. Remember what the Bible says.** Read aloud Psalm 145:3 again. **God is worthy of our praise. We can praise God every day—just by looking at all the wonderful things around us!**

Preschool
PLAY POINTER

You may want to bring in a storybook that has a picture of a king. Point out that people bow when they see the king, and they say nice things about the king. Be sure that children understand that a king is a very special and important person.

Royal Ribbon Parade

GROWING CLOSER: We can honor God.

KEY VERSE: "The crowds that went ahead of him and those that followed shouted, 'Hosanna to the Son of David! Blessed is he who comes in the name of the Lord!' " (Matthew 21:9a).

SUPPLIES: a Bible, drinking straws, purple curling ribbon, tape, scissors

The Game:

Before children arrive, cut several pieces of curling ribbon into three-foot lengths.

Say: **One of the most exciting events is a parade. Shake your hands in the air if you like parades.** Pause while children respond. **Jesus was part of a parade, and people waved palm branches and laid their colorful coats on the road for his donkey to step on. They were excited to see Jesus, and they wanted to show how much they loved him. They treated Jesus like a king! Listen to what the Bible says.** Read aloud Matthew 21:9a from an easy-to-understand Bible translation. **Today, we're going to make royal ribbon streamers to help us celebrate our King Jesus!**

Show children how to tape pieces of curling ribbon to the end of a straw. As children work, talk about the royal color of purple. Explain that kings and queens often wore purple to show that they were royal (or special) people. Say: **Jesus is the King of kings, so we want to use purple ribbons as we praise him.**

When each child has a ribbon streamer, have children form two lines, facing each other. Say: **Let's pretend that we were there that day when Jesus rode his donkey into Jerusalem. Remember, the people started to worship Jesus for being their king. They shouted, "Hosanna! Blessed is he who comes in the name of the Lord!" Let's do that, too.**

Lead children in waving their ribbon streamers and shouting, "Hosanna! Blessed is he who comes in the name of the Lord!" Then teach children the following song to the tune of "Ten Little Indians."

Preschool PLAY POINTER

You may want to read this story from a picture book so children can see how the people laid their cloaks and palm branches on the road for Jesus.

Let's all honor and praise Jesus.
Let's all honor and praise Jesus.
Let's all honor and praise Jesus.
Jesus is our King!

A Present for God

GROWING CLOSER: We can give God good gifts.

KEY VERSE: "Therefore, my dear brothers, stand firm. Let nothing move you. Always give yourselves fully to the work of the Lord, because you know that your labor in the Lord is not in vain" (1 Corinthians 15:58).

SUPPLIES: crayons and a box wrapped in plain, white paper

The Game:

Have kids sit in a circle, and place the gift box and crayons in the center of the circle. Ask:

• **What is the best present you've ever received?**

• **Why did someone give that gift to you?**

Say: **We give presents for lots of reasons—birthdays, Christmas, or sometimes just because we love a person. God is our King, and we can show our love for God by giving him presents, too.** Ask:

• **What kind of presents would you give God?**

Say: **Let's pretend this box is a present we're giving to God. We're going to give God a special present by giving him our love. To show that we're giving ourselves to God, we'll pass the box around and let each person put his or her hand print on the paper. Then tell something that you can do to show your love for God.**

Preschool
PLAY POINTER

This is a great time to lead children in a time of praise and worship through singing. Explain that singing is just one way to give a gift to God, our King.

Begin by outlining the shape of your hand on the box, and then tell something you can do to show how much you love God. Pass the box around the circle, and let children add their hand prints while they share. (If you have more than ten children in your group, you'll want to have two boxes going around the circle simultaneously.)

When everyone has added a hand print, say: **The Bible tells us to do everything as if we were doing it for God. That means that all our actions can be like gifts to God. God is pleased when we're kind or helpful, or when we say how much we love him. Let's give a special gift to God, our King, with this prayer.**

Lead children in the following prayer:

God, I give you my voice as I shout and sing. *(Hold hands to mouth.)*
I'll praise and thank my God and king! *(Raise hands.)*
I give you my hands when I serve and hug. *(Clap hands, then hug self.)*
I want everyone to know your love. *(Open arms wide.)*
God, I give you my feet. Please help me, though *(stomp feet)*
To run and walk where you want me to go. *(Walk in place.)*
Most of all, God, I give you my heart. *(Cross hands over heart.)*
Take all that I am and not just one part. *(Open arms wide.)*
Amen.

Praise Parade

GROWING CLOSER: God is worthy of our praise.
KEY VERSE: "I will exalt you, my God the King; I will praise your name for ever and ever" (Psalm 145:1).
SUPPLIES: a Bible, one colorful scarf or streamer for each child

The Game:

Read Psalm 145:1 aloud. Say: **The Bible tells us that God is our King.** Ask:

• **How do people treat a king?**
• **Why do people do those things?**

Say: **In Bible times, people celebrated and cheered for their kings. They waved palm branches or colorful pieces of cloth. They wanted to show that they loved their leader. It was kind of like the way we cheer at football or** basketball games today. Let's cheer for God with this fun game of Follow the Leader.

Distribute scarves and play some upbeat praise music while you lead children in the following actions:

Walk in a circle.
Lift your arms up and shout "Hooray!"
Wave scarf overhead.
Shout "We love God!"
Wave scarf around your feet.
Wave scarf around in circle with arm straight (like a windmill).
Run in circle waving scarf.
Shout "Praise God!"
March in place and wave scarf out to the side.
Shout "Yea, God!"

Have children sit down, while you collect the scarves. Ask:
• **How is God our leader?**
• **What are some things we can praise God for?**
• **How can we praise God each day?**
Read aloud Psalm 145:1 again. Say: **God is our King—our leader. We can praise him and cheer for him every day. We can thank God for being a good and kind leader for us. God is worthy of our praise.**

Praise Scavenger Hunt

GROWING CLOSER: We can praise God in many ways.

KEY VERSE: "For the Lord takes delight in his people; he crowns the humble with salvation" (Psalm 149:4).

SUPPLIES: a Bible, one balloon, four slips of paper, pen or pencil, tape, a tambourine or other instrument, a colorful scarf, smiley-face stickers

The Game:

Before children arrive, set up this simple scavenger hunt. First, write "Shout 'hallelujah' and look for the tambourine" on a slip of paper. Then place the paper inside the balloon, and blow up the balloon. Write "Shake me and shout 'God is awesome!' and look for the scarf" on another slip of paper, then tape the paper to the tambourine. On another slip of paper, write "Dance with me, shout 'God is great!' and find the happy faces." Tape that slip of paper to a colorful scarf. Finally, write "Put me on your clothes, smile, and say 'God is good' on the last slip of paper. Tape the paper to the sheet of smiley-faced stickers. Hide all the items except for the balloon.

Form groups of five, and give one child on each team a balloon. Say: **We're going on a praise scavenger hunt. On a scavenger hunt, you follow clues and search for things. On a praise scavenger hunt, we'll follow clues that tell us new ways to praise God, our King. Let each person on your team have a turn praising God with the items you find. We'll start by popping this balloon.** Let the child holding the balloon find a fun way to pop the balloon, either by stepping on it or sitting on it. Read aloud the clue, and help children search for the next item. Continue the search until children have found the smiley-faced stickers. Then gather everyone in a circle. Ask:

Preschool
PLAY POINTER

For every five children, set up another identical scavenger hunt. You'll need a teen or adult helper to accompany children through the hunt and to read the clues.

- **What was it like to praise God in this scavenger hunt?**
- **What was your favorite way to praise God?**

Read aloud Psalm 149:4 from an easy-to-understand Bible translation. Say: **God loves to hear our praises. We can sing our praises. We can shout our praises or dance to praise God. God is King—he is worthy of our praise and celebration.**

Many Ways to Praise

GROWING CLOSER: God is worthy of our praise.

KEY VERSE: "The trumpeters and singers joined in unison, as with one voice, to give praise and thanks to the Lord. Accompanied by trumpets, cymbals and other instruments, they raised their voices in praise to the Lord and sang: 'He is good; his love endures forever' " (2 Chronicles 5:13).

SUPPLIES: a Bible

The Game:

Have children form a circle. Say: **God is our King—that means he's important and powerful. The Bible tells us to praise God, our King.** Ask:

• **What does it mean to praise God?**

• **How can you praise God?**

Say: **When we praise God, we're saying how much we love God and how great he is. The Bible tells us that there are many ways to praise God.** Read aloud 2 Chronicles 5:13. Continue: **God is King, and we're going to praise him with our voices by singing a song, and with our bodies by doing fun motions.**

Lead children in singing the following song to the tune of "London Bridge." While singing, do the action indicated by the words of the verse.

We can praise in many ways, many ways, many ways.
We can praise in many ways.
God is our King.
We can lift our hands up high, hands up high, hands up high.
We can lift our hands up high.
God is our King.
We can clap our hands like this, hands like this, hands like this.
We can clap our hands like this.
God is our King.
We can march around and round, round and round, round and round.
We can march around and round.
God is our King.
We can bow our heads down low, heads down low, heads down low.
We can bow our heads down low.
God is our King.
We can shout, "I love you," "I love you," "I love you."
We can shout, "I love you."
God is our King.

Allow children to repeat any favorite verses or create their own verses that tell more ways to praise God.

Banners for God

GROWING CLOSER: God is King, and we praise our king.

KEY VERSE: "We will shout for joy when you are victorious and will lift up our banners in the name of our God" (Psalm 20:5a).

SUPPLIES: construction paper (8½ X 11-inch), scissors, crayons or markers, crepe paper, straws, stapler, a chair, jingle bells (optional)

The Game:

Before children arrive, cut the construction paper in half, diagonally, to create triangles. These are your banners. You'll need one banner per child.

Ask: • **What are some things that you see at football or basketball games?**

Say: **At sporting events, people sometimes bring signs or banners to show that they really like their team. Today we'll make banners to show how great God is.**

Allow children to color their banners. While children are working, come around and staple the short side of each banner to a straw to make a handle. You may even want to let children attach jingle bells so their banners make noise! When everyone has made a banner, say: **God is King of the whole world and over all of heaven. The Bible tells us that in heaven, God has a beautiful throne and all the angels and people worship him. Let's use our banners today and pretend we are in heaven, standing before God's throne, worshipping with the angels.**

Set a chair in the middle of the room, and drape crepe paper over it to represent God's throne. Say: **We'll go around the circle and shout out praises to God. You might praise God for something he's given you, like your family or your home. Or you might praise God for what a great God he is and how much you love him. After each person praises God,** we'll all shout, **"God is great! God is good! Lift your banners high!" and wave our banners. Let's practice our shout of praise together.** Lead children in shouting several times, "God is great! God is good! Lift your banners high!" Then start the activity by saying a praise phrase and leading children in shouting their praises together. Go around the circle and let each child give a praise.

When everyone has had a turn, say: **God is King of everything, and he will be praised forever and ever. Take your banners home with you and use them to praise God again!**

GOD IS
Listening

"This is the confidence

we have in approaching God:

that if we ask anything

according to his will,

he hears us."

(1 John 5:14)

The Listening Stick

GROWING CLOSER: God is always ready to listen to us.

KEY VERSE: "I call on the Lord in my distress, and he answers me" (Psalm 120:1).

SUPPLIES: a decorative pencil for each child, or some other object that can represent a listening stick

The Game:

Use chairs to form a circle, and have children sit down. Place an empty chair next to you. Hold up a pencil and say: **This pencil is going to be our listening stick. The person holding the listening stick is the only person who may talk. When that person is talking, the rest of us must listen quietly.**

Walk over to one child and ask:

• **What is the most fun thing you did this week?**

Hand the child the stick, and let him or her answer. Use non-verbal cues to remind the other children that they must listen. When the child has finished answering, take the stick and go to another child. Ask him or her the same question. Continue until each child has had a turn to hold the stick and share a response.

Then say: **In the Bible book of Psalms, it says that God answers our prayers—that God listens to us. We're going to pretend that God is sitting in this chair.** Motion to the empty chair. **Think about what you would say to God if you could see him sitting in this chair, just like you see your other friends sitting here.**

Hold the listening stick, look at the chair, and tell God one thing, such as "Thank you for loving me." Be sure your comment is simple enough for preschoolers to model. Then pass the stick to the child nearest you, and let him or her talk to God. When each child has had a turn, gather in the middle of the circle and let everyone touch the stick. Lead children in shouting "Yea, God!"

Preschool
PLAY POINTER

As you pass the stick around the circle, children will discover how to take part in a sentence prayer. This experience may be new for some children, so remember to be flexible and allow them a moment to think about what they'll say.

Distribute pencils or "listening sticks" to each child. Say: **God listens to you all the time, whether you have a listening stick or not. But this stick can remind you that God is always listening to you. He is always paying attention when you talk to him.**

Roll-a-Prayer

GROWING CLOSER: We can pray in many ways.
KEY VERSE: "I will listen to what God the Lord will say" (Psalm 85:8a).
SUPPLIES: a small, square tissue box; paper; tape; markers

The Game:

Before class, make a game cube by wrapping the tissue box in plain paper. Next draw one of the following pictures on each side of the cube:

Praise: a stick figure with arms raised

Song: music notes

Ask: a stick figure with hands together in prayer

Thanks: a heart

Listen: a happy face with large, exaggerated ears

Sorry: a sad face

Gather children in a circle and say: **Show me what you do when you're excited about something.** Pause. **Now show me what you do when you're sorry for something you've done.** Pause. **Show me how you act when someone gives you a great gift.** Pause. **Show me what you might do if you really wanted something.** Pause. **We act in different ways to show how we're feeling. We can talk to God in different ways, too.**

Hold up the cube and say: **This is our prayer cube. Each of the pictures shows a different way we can talk to God.**

Point to the figure raising its arms. **This shows someone cele-brating or praising. When the cube lands with this picture face-up, we'll all praise God by raising our arms and cheering, "Yea, God!"** Briefly explain each of the other actions, as follows:

Song: Sing "Yes, Jesus loves me! The Bible tells me so."

Ask: Let a child pray for a need.

Thanks: Say, "Thanks, God, for _____!" and let children shout out things they're thankful for.

Listen: Cup your hands around your ears and listen for ten seconds.

Sorry: Bow heads and say, "God, we're sorry."

Say: **Let's take turns tossing the cube in the middle of our circle. When the cube stops, we'll see which picture is face-up. Then we'll all talk to God—or listen to God—in that way. OK?**

Let children take turns tossing the cube and doing the appropriate actions. You'll need to cue children in to the actions for the first few turns. After everyone has had at least one turn, say: **There are so many ways to talk to God. We can be loud as we sing songs and praise God, or we can be quiet as we listen to what God has to say. But whenever we talk to God, we know that he's listening to every word we say.**

Closer and Closer

GROWING CLOSER: God wants to be close to us.

KEY VERSE: " 'You are my witnesses,' declares the Lord, 'and my servant whom I have chosen, so that you may know and believe me and understand that I am he. Before me no god was formed, nor will there be one after me' " (Isaiah 43:10).

SUPPLIES: none

The Game:

Have children line up at one end of the room. Stand across the room from them. Ask:

• **What do you like to do when you're with your friends?**

• **How do you stay in touch with friends or family who are far away?**

Say: **It can be hard to be apart from people that we love. You miss them very much. In this game, you'll try to get closer to me. Each person will get a turn to name something to talk with God about. You might say, "I can talk to God about my friends" or "I can tell God about my day at school." Then, think of a fun way to get closer to me. You might hop, skip, crawl, jog, march, or scoot all the way to me. Try to do something different from anyone else.**

As each child reaches you, welcome him or her with a big hug or a high five. When everyone has reached you, gather in a circle. Say: **God loves us so much that he wants to be close to us. He wants to hear what we're thinking and what we're doing. He wants to help us when we have problems. Talking to God is just one way to know God better and grow closer to him.**

Form a tight circle and pray: **Dear God, we're glad that you want to be close to us. We want to be close to you, too. Help us spend time with you so we can know you better. Amen.**

Preschool
PLAY POINTER

This is a neat activity to use as a class opener, since it reminds children that God is present in their classroom. It's also a great way to hear what's on children's minds and a good time to affirm them with a big hug!

Listening Carefully

GROWING CLOSER: God is never too busy for us.

KEY VERSE: "The Lord will keep you from all harm—he will watch over your life; the Lord will watch over your coming and going both now and forevermore" (Psalm 121:7-8).

SUPPLIES: none

The Game:

Have the children stand, facing you. Say: **We're going to see if you can do lots of things at the same time. Watch what I do, then you do the same thing. Ready?**

Start by marching in place. Keep marching, then begin patting your head with your left hand. Keep both actions going, and rub your stomach in a circular motion with your right hand. Keep all three going and make silly faces. Continue for as long as you can, then stop for a laughter break! Ask:

• **What was it like to do so many things at once?**

Say: **Let's try another game. This one is called Simon Says. Follow my instructions as long as I first say, "Simon Says." If I don't say, "Simon Says," don't follow the instructions. OK?**

Play a few rounds of Simon Says. Then say: **You can all be Simon now, and I'll try to do what you say. I think I can handle all your directions at once, so go ahead.** Let the children give several instructions simultaneously and try to follow them. Be sure to make several mistakes along the way! After a few minutes, end the game and ask:

• **Did I do a very good job of following all your directions? Why not?**

• **Did you think I would be able to do everything at once?**

Say: **We can't do lots and lots of things at once, but God can! God is never too busy for us. He will always have time to listen when we talk with him.**

Preschool ● PLAY POINTER

Young children may have difficulty thinking of actions for you to do. If so, you can prompt them by asking, "What if Simon said to walk on my knees?" or another silly instruction.

A Pin Drop

GROWING CLOSER: God is listening.
KEY VERSE: "The Lord is far from the wicked but he hears the prayer of the righteous" (Proverbs 15:29).
SUPPLIES: a pin; various items such as a cotton ball, a paper clip, jingle bells, a facial tissue, a Ping-Pong ball, coins, a pencil, a crayon, chalk, plastic cup, silverware

The Game:

Before the game, seat children around a table. Say: **When it's very, very quiet, some people say, "It was so quiet, you could hear a pin drop." Let's hear how quiet that would be.** Have children sit quietly while you drop a pin on the table. **Wow! That didn't make very much noise at all! We had to listen pretty closely to hear it.**

We're going to play a listening game. First, close your eyes tightly, and place your hands over them. It's important that you can't see what item I drop on the table. Listen carefully to the sound when I drop something, and see if you can guess what the object is by the sound it makes.

After children have their eyes closed and hands over their eyes, begin the game. Drop objects such as jingle bells, a Ping-Pong ball, a spoon, or a coin. Then try more difficult objects such as chalk, a plastic cup, a cotton ball, or paper clips. Pause after each item, and allow children to try to guess the item. Then let children open their eyes to see what the item was. When you've dropped about seven items, let children open their eyes. Ask:

• **How did you know what the items where?**

Say: **You needed to listen very carefully to know what was making those different sounds. God listens very carefully to us, too. He knows each of our voices and is always ready to listen when we pray. God loves the times we talk with him. It doesn't have to be quiet for God to hear us, either. God can always hear us, whether we whisper, shout, or just talk.**

God Understands

GROWING CLOSER: God understands everyone.

KEY VERSE: "After this I looked and there before me was a great multitude that no one could count, from every nation, tribe, people and language, standing before the throne and in front of the Lamb" (Revelation 7:9a).

SUPPLIES: none

The Game:

For this version of the game Telephone, have the children form two lines of equal length. (If you have fewer than ten children, form one line) Say: **I'm going to whisper a message to the first person in line. That person will whisper the message to the next person in line. We'll keep passing the message down the line. If you're not sure what someone said to you, just whisper what you *think* you heard. The last person in line will tell the message that he or she heard. Ready?**

Whisper the phrase, "God understands everyone" to the first person in line. Have children pass the message down the line, until the last person says the message aloud. Say: **The message that I whispered was "God understands everyone."** Ask:

• **How was my message different from the message that we ended up with?**

• **Why did the message get mixed up?**

• **Have you ever heard someone speak in a different language? What was that like?**

Say: **Sometimes people use big words, and we can't understand what they're talking about. Other times, people speak a different language, so we can't understand them. But God understands everyone! It doesn't matter if we use big words, small words, or if we speak in a different language. The Bible tells us that God can always understand our words. That means that people everywhere can praise and love the same God!**

Preschool PLAY POINTER

If children successfully pass the message, congratulate them! Ask how they managed to succeed in passing the message. Talk about how important it is to listen carefully, and assure them that God always listens to us carefully.

GOD IS
Loving

"No, the Father himself loves you
because you have loved me
and have believed that I came from God."
(John 16:27)

Sheep and Shepherds

GROWING CLOSER: God is like a good shepherd.

KEY VERSE: "He tends his flock like a shepherd: He gathers the lambs in his arms and carries them close to his heart; he gently leads those that have young" (Isaiah 40:11).

SUPPLIES: two chairs, masking tape, and blindfolds for at least half of the children

The Game:

Before children arrive, make a "gate" by placing two chairs back to back, about two feet apart. Be sure the chairs are close enough so that only one child at a time can walk through the gate. Then use the masking tape to make a path that winds around the room and ends at the gate. (If you can't place masking tape on your floor, use a length of rope to delineate your path.)

Form pairs, and blindfold one child in each pair. Explain that the blindfolded children are Sheep and their partners are Shepherds. Say: **Shepherds will guide their Sheep around the room, then through the gate that leads to the sheep pen. It's important that our Shepherds are kind and gentle, being careful not to let the Sheep wander away or bump into anything. Ready?**

As you lead the Shepherds along the path, encourage the Sheep to have fun making "sheep noises." When all the Sheep are in the pen, have children trade roles and play again. Then gather in the sheep pen, and congratulate all the Sheep and Shepherds for a job well-done. Ask:

• **What did it feel like to wear a blindfold?**

• **How did your Shepherd lead you?**

Preschool
PLAY POINTER

Some children may be uncomfortable having their eyes covered. If so, simply allow them to close their eyes or look at the ceiling.

Say: **Real sheep can see, but when they're in the middle of their flock, they can't see anything but the other sheep. They have to trust the shepherd to tell them where to go.** Ask:

• **What does a shepherd do to take care of his sheep?**

Say: **The Bible teaches us that God is like a good shepherd to us. We can't see him, but he is always with us, helping and protecting us. God lovingly cares for us, just as a shepherd cares for his sheep.**

Bursts of Anger

GROWING CLOSER: God is gentle.

KEY VERSE: "You are a forgiving God, gracious and compassionate, slow to anger and abounding in love" (Nehemiah 9:17b).

SUPPLIES: at least twelve inflated balloons in two or three colors; two or three boxes or laundry baskets; large pin or other sharp object; soft objects such as hand towels, cotton swabs, or rolled-up paper

The Game:

Scatter the balloons in the middle of the floor, and place a basket or box on opposite sides of the room. Form two or three groups of children, and give each group a few soft objects. Assign a color to each group, then say: **It's your job to gather all of the balloons of your color, using the objects I've given you. You may not touch the balloons with your hands or feet. You'll need to put all your balloons in your group's basket. Try to gather as many balloons as possible, without popping any. Ready?**

As the game progresses, encourage kids to be gentle as they move their balloons into the baskets. When all the balloons are in baskets, congratulate children and gather them in a circle. Ask:

• **What was hard about this game?**

• **How did you keep your balloons from breaking?**

Hold up a large pin or other sharp object. Ask:

Preschool ⚬
PLAY POINTER

Pieces of popped balloons are a choking hazard. Be sure to quickly pick up any balloon pieces and throw them away.

• **What might have happened if I'd given you something like this to move your balloons with?**

Say: **When we have something that might break, we can be careful and gentle with it. God treats us with kindness and gentleness, just as you treated your balloons. Even when we do wrong things, God is never rough or mean to us. He loves us gently.**

Bandage Game

GROWING CLOSER: God is the good physician.
KEY VERSE: "Heal me, O Lord, and I will be healed; save me and I will be saved, for you are the one I praise" (Jeremiah 17:14).
SUPPLIES: a Bible, one brightly colored adhesive bandage per child, index cards, magazines, scissors, glue

The Game:

Before the game, prepare flashcards from the index cards and magazines. Cut photos of knees, elbows, wrists, arms, chins, and other body parts. Glue a picture of a body part on each index card. Be sure to make enough cards for each child to have one.

Distribute brightly colored adhesive bandages. You may need to help children unwrap the bandages. Instruct the children to hold their bandages. Ask:

• **What are these used for?**

• **How does a cut or scrape feel after you put a bandage on it?**

Say: **I have a stack of cards that show different parts of our bodies. I'll give each person a card. Look at your card and the body part that is shown there, then put your bandage on that part of your body. For example, if I got the card that had a nose on it, I'd put my bandage on my nose. Ready?**

Distribute the cards and offer assistance to any children who may need it. When everyone is wearing a bandage, read aloud Jeremiah 17:14. Ask:

• **When you fall down and get hurt, how does God help?**

• **What are some other ways that God helps heal our hurts?**

Say: **The Bible says that God can heal us. That means God can heal our hurts on the outside—like scraped knees and bruised elbows. But it also means that God can heal us on the inside—like when we're sad or get our feelings hurt. God cares for us and wants to make us feel better. Today, when someone asks why you're wearing a bandage, you can tell the person that it reminds you that God cares for us!**

Preschool PLAY POINTER

Preschoolers *love* bandages! For extra fun, provide several bandages for each child, and play this game two or three times. Children will have many reminders of God's healing hand in their lives.

The Highway of Holiness

GROWING CLOSER: God lovingly watches over us.

KEY VERSE: "And a highway will be there; it will be called the Way of Holiness" (Isaiah 35:8a).

SUPPLIES: large sheets of construction paper, black markers, crayons or washable markers, stuffed animals of "ferocious" beasts such as tigers and bears

The Game:

Say: **The Bible book of Isaiah tells us about a road that is just for people who love God. This road is called the Way of Holiness. "Holiness" means "goodness." When people walk on the Way of Holiness, God keeps them safe. Let's make a pretend road to see what that might be like.**

Show the children how to stand on the construction paper and draw around their feet. Let them color the footprints with crayons or washable markers. Say: **Now we'll make our Way of Holiness.**

Have children set down their footprint papers to make a winding path. If you have fewer than ten children, let children make two sheets of paper, to create a path that stretches across the room. At the end of the path, place a sheet of paper with the word "God" written on it. Be sure to tell children what the paper says. Let children place stuffed animals alongside the road, but not touching the road.

Say: **As you take turns walking on the Way of Holiness, notice the wild animals near the path. Imagine what it would be like if they were real lions, tigers, and bears.** Let children take turns walking along the path, then gather children at the end of the path. Ask:

• **What would have happened if the lions and tigers were real?**

• **What other things are you afraid of?**

• **What can you do when you're afraid?**

Say: **The Bible tells us that God watches over us. Even when we're afraid or it seems like bad things might happen, God is watching us and will take care of us. When we love and follow God, it's like we're on the Way of Holiness and God keeps bad things away from us.**

Let children take home their piece of the Way of Holiness as a reminder to keep their feet on "God's path."

Preschool
PLAY POINTER

This is a super opportunity for children to use their imaginations. They'll have a wonderful time pretending that the animals are real!

Animals Everywhere!

GROWING CLOSER: God watches over us.

KEY VERSE: " 'Am I only a God nearby,' declares the Lord, 'and not a God far away? Can anyone hide in secret places so that I cannot see him?' " (Jeremiah 23:23-24a).

SUPPLIES: stuffed animals, at least one for each child

The Game:

Form a circle and give each child a stuffed animal, then say: **Some of these animals are a little shy. They want to hide. Some of these animals are wild and want to run away where we can't find them. When I say "go," run and hide your animal in a good place. Then come back to our circle. Go!**

When everyone is gathered again, ask:

• **Do you think anyone would be able to find the animal that you hid? Why or why not?**

Say: **Let's see if we can round up all these animals that are hiding. I'll say "go" again, and you'll try to find someone else's animal and bring it back to the circle. Ready? Go!**

When all the animals have been rounded up, play the game again. Encourage children to look for new places to hide the animals. After several rounds, ask:

• **How hard was it to find the animals?**

• **How did you feel when you found a hidden animal?**

Say: **The Bible tells us that God is always watching over us. There's no place that we can go where God won't see us. It's impossible to hide from God. God is always watching over us, because God cares about us.**

• **What's it like to know that God is always with you?**

• **When are some times when you _really_ want God nearby?**

Say: **Hold your stuffed animal close in a big hug while we pray.** Lead children in a prayer, similar to this one. Pray: **Dear God, thank you for caring for us and watching over us. It's nice to know that you are always nearby. We are glad to know that there is no place we can go, where you can't find us. Amen.**

You may want to share about a time when you were lost or _felt_ alone. Most children have had similar experiences, and it will be reassuring to hear that adults may feel that way some-times, too.

Let Us Love

GROWING CLOSER: God is caring.

KEY VERSE: "Dear friends, let us love one another, for love comes from God" (1 John 4:7a).

SUPPLIES: a teddy bear or other stuffed animal, a small paper heart or heart sticker for each child, safety pins or transparent tape, a piece of cloth or construction paper (If you have a stuffed animal that already has a pocket, you won't need the tape, pins, paper, or cloth.)

The Game:

Before the game, create a pocket on the stuffed animal by taping or pinning the fabric piece or paper to the animal. Be sure the pocket is large enough for children to reach into and pull out the paper hearts. Place the hearts into the pocket.

Have children form a circle. Bring the stuffed animal to the circle. Ask:

· **What does it mean to care about someone?**

Say: **When we care about people, we love them, help them, and want good things to happen to them. God is caring.** Ask:

· **How does God show that he cares for us?**

Say: **The Bible tells us that God cares for us by giving us food to eat and water to drink. God cares for us by listening when we talk to him. God shows that he cares by sending Jesus to take away our sins. God also wants us to care for others.** Hold up the teddy bear. **This teddy bear will help us think of ways to do that.**

Let's pretend that this teddy bear is a friend of ours. Inside his pocket are little hearts. As we pass the bear around the circle, each person will take a turn telling how he or she can care for the bear. After you've told one way to care for the bear, you can take a heart from the bear. That will be his way of thanking you for being so caring.

Start the game by saying, "I will care for teddy by..." then name a way you could care for the bear. Suggest ideas to the children such as hugging the bear, tying his shoe, giving the bear a drink of water, saying kind words to the bear, or giving him a bandage when he scrapes his knee. Encourage children to be as imaginative as they wish.

After everyone has a heart, say: **Take the heart home and the next time someone in your family cares for you, give that person the heart and say "thank you" just like teddy!**

Hug-a-Bug

GROWING CLOSER: We can love others the way God loves us.

KEY VERSE: "Dear friends, let us love one another, for love comes from God" (1 John 4:7a).

SUPPLIES: masking tape and a ball

The Game:

Before children arrive, use masking tape to make a large X in the middle of the playing area.

Gather children around the X and say: **God loves us so much! The Bible even tells us that love comes from God.**

Read aloud 1 John 4:7a, then continue: **Let's show each other God's love by playing a hugging game called Hug-a-Bug. I'll toss the ball to someone, and that person will be the "Bug." The Bug will take the ball and stand on the X in the middle. Then the rest of us will go into the middle of the circle and hug the Bug. The Bug will toss the ball to someone else, who will become the new Bug.**

Begin tossing the ball, then leading children in a group hug. When everyone has had a turn to be the Bug, say: **Now that we've all been hugged, let's learn a song about God's love.** Lead children in singing the following song, to the tune of "This Old Man." (You may want to toss the ball around the circle while children are singing. Whoever is holding the ball at the end of the song will be the center of a group hug!)

Preschool ◉
PLAY POINTER

Some children may be uncomfortable being hugged closely by many new children. If so, allow children to simply give high fives. The loving, affirming message will still get through!

**I love God.
God loves me.
That's the way it ought to be!
God will give me love,
And I'll pass it on to you!
Won't you say you love God, too?**

Ask: • **How does God show his love to you?**
• **How does God feel when we love others?**
• **What would it be like if everyone showed God's love?**

Say: **God is loving. In fact, love comes from God. We can show God's love to others in so many ways. This week, practice the Hug-a-Bug game with your friends and family. It's a great way to let others feel God's love!**

A Gentle Shepherd

GROWING CLOSER: God takes care of us.
KEY VERSE: "The Lord is my shepherd, I shall not be in want" (Psalm 23:1).
SUPPLIES: a Bible, masking tape, cotton balls

The Game:

Before the game, make several masking tape circles (about twelve-inches in diameter) at one end of the room. You'll need one circle for each group of five children.

Have children form groups of no more than five. Then instruct groups to line up at one end of the room, opposite the masking tape circles. Hold up a cotton ball and say: **Let's pretend this cotton ball is a fluffy, white sheep. You're all shepherds who need to get your sheep into the sheep pen at the other end of the room. Shepherds need to be loving and gentle with their sheep, so you'll move your sheep by gently blowing on them.**

Demonstrate how to blow a cotton ball "sheep" across the room. Then continue: **I'll give each group a handful of sheep. You'll take turns guiding your sheep into the sheep pen across from you. After you've put a sheep in the pen, run back and gently tap the next person and let him or her guide a sheep.**

Distribute cotton balls, then say "Go" to begin the game. When all the sheep are in a pen, gather children in a circle. Say: **These were just pretend sheep.** Ask:

• **What might happen if real sheep were left out in the wild overnight?**

• **What does a shepherd need to do to take care of his or her sheep?**

Say: **The Bible tells us that God is like a shepherd, and we are like his sheep.** Read aloud Psalm 23:1-3, then continue: **God is loving. Just as a shepherd loves and cares for his sheep, God loves and cares for us. Just as you gently blew your cotton ball sheep into their pens, God gently protects and guides us.**

Give each child a cotton ball to take home as a reminder that God is loving, just like a shepherd.

Touch Gently

GROWING CLOSER: God is gentle to us.

KEY VERSE: "We were gentle among you, like a mother caring for her little children" (1 Thessalonians 2:7).

SUPPLIES: a doll or stuffed animal for each child, a scarf or facial tissue for each child

The Game:

Have children form a circle. Say: **Hold up one finger. Now, use just that one finger to tap somebody on the shoulder. Tap very lightly and softly. That kind of tap is being gentle.** Give each child a scarf or facial tissue.

Say: **Now, wave your scarf gently in the air over your head. Make soft, gentle circles with your scarf.** Lead children in using their scarves to touch their toes or knees gently, to softly brush against someone's back, or to lightly tickle a friend's face. Ask:

• **What does gentleness feel like?**

• **Who do you know that is gentle? How does that person show gentleness?**

Say: **God is loving and gentle to us. Listen to how God's helpers treated people in the Bible.** Read aloud 1 Thessalonians 2:7, then ask:

• **Why do you think they treated people gently?**

• **How does a mother treat a baby?**

Say: **God is loving, just as a mother is loving to her little baby. Even when we grow up to be big people, God will still love us tenderly. God wants us to be loving and gentle to others, too. Let's practice that right now.**

Give each child a doll or stuffed animal. Let children wrap their "babies" in the scarves, then rock, cuddle, or speak softly to their babies. Lead children in softly singing this song to the tune of "Jesus Loves Me."

Preschool
PLAY POINTER

If time allows, have a mother bring in a newborn baby. Let her tell about how gently she must hold and touch the baby. This "hands-on" example will be powerful for children.

God is gentle, this I know.
He will love me as I grow.
Softly, softly God calls me.
God's little child I'll always be.
Yes, God is gentle.
Yes, God is gentle.
Yes, God is gentle.
The Bible tells me so.

GOD IS
Powerful

"No one is like you, O Lord;

you are great,

and your name is mighty in power."

(Jeremiah 10:6)

Stronger Than Anything

GROWING CLOSER: God watches over us.

KEY VERSE: "When you pass through the waters, I will be with you; and when you pass through the rivers, they will not sweep over you. When you walk through the fire, you will not be burned; the flames will not set you ablaze. For I am the Lord, your God" (Isaiah 43:2-3a).

SUPPLIES: none

The Game:

Ask: • **What are some things that are scary for you?**

• **What do you do when you're feeling scared?**

Say: **The Bible tells us that God is powerful enough to protect us from anything. God is always watching over us. This game will help us remember that God is more powerful than the things that scare us.**

When I say "Go," you'll all run from me, trying not to get tagged. If I tag you, stop and "freeze" into a statue until another person tags you and says, "God protects you" or "God is stronger than anything."

Play the game for a few minutes, then choose a few children to be "It" and tag others. Be sure to remind children to say, "God protects you" or "God is stronger than anything" whenever they "un-tag" someone. After a few minutes, gather children together. Ask:

• **How do you feel, now that you know God is watching over you?**

• **What can you do when you're feeling scared?**

Say: **God protects us wherever we go. He is more powerful than the most scary thing we can imagine! We don't need to be frozen with fear!**

Preschool
PLAY POINTER

Some preschoolers face very real fears. Be sensitive to abusive home situations and other experiences children may have had. Gently explain that sometimes God uses people like Sunday school teachers or other relatives to help us out of scary situations.

Lost at Sea

GROWING CLOSER: God protects us.

KEY VERSE: "Who is this? He commands even the winds and the water, and they obey him" (Luke 8:25b).

SUPPLIES: a Bible, one plastic soda bottle cap for each child, water, one 9X13-inch pan for every three children

The Game:

Before the game, fill several pans half-full with water. (You'll need one pan for every three children.)

Form groups of no more than three children. Hold up a plastic bottle cap and say: **Pretend this bottle cap is a boat and the pan of water is a huge lake. You're going to be the mighty wind that blows the boat from one side of the lake to the other.**

Show children how to put the bottle cap in the water and blow it across to the other side of the pan. Show children how to blow the boats gently, then more forcefully so they can see the effect that different kinds of wind have on a boat. Then say: **I'll give each person a boat. Take turns blowing your boat across the lake, then let the next person have a turn.**

Distribute bottle cap "boats," and say "Go" to begin the game. When everyone has had a turn to blow the boats across the "lake" several times, gather children in a circle. Ask:

• **What happened to your boats when you blew a hard wind on them?**

• **What happens to real boats when they're in a mighty wind?**

• **How would you feel if you were in a boat during a powerful storm?**

Say: **The Bible tells us that God can command even the wind and water.** Read aloud Luke 8:22-25 from an easy-to-understand Bible translation or from a Bible storybook. Then say: **God is powerful and he protects us. Just as you were able to blow the little boat hard or softly, God can command**

even the wind and water. Read aloud Luke 8:22-25 from an easy-to-understand Bible translation or from a Bible storybook. Then say: **God is powerful and he protects us. Just as you were able to blow the little boat hard or softly, God can command the wind and weather and make it do what he wants. God can protect us from scary things.**

Give each child a bottle cap boat as a reminder that God can protect us when we're afraid.

Muscle Movers

GROWING CLOSER: God is more powerful than we are.

KEY VERSE: "O great and powerful God, whose name is the Lord Almighty, great are your purposes and mighty are your deeds" (Jeremiah 32:18b-19a).

SUPPLIES: a Bible, several strong packing boxes large enough for a child to fit inside (Large rectangular laundry baskets work well, too.)

The Game:

Before the game begins, clear a large area on the floor for children to push one another across the room in boxes. Line up the boxes at one end of the open area.

Say: **Today we're going to learn a little about muscles and a lot about Gods' mighty strength. It's amazing how much you are growing every day! As you eat good food, play, and rest, God is making your body grow healthy and strong. Sometimes you might even think that you are as strong as your big brother or your mommy! Let's play a game that tests our muscles. In this game, you'll use your mighty muscles to move your friends across the room.**

Form pairs and have them line up behind the boxes. Explain that one partner will sit inside the box while the other partner pushes the box across the room. When partners reach the other side of the room, they'll trade places and push the box back to the starting line.

Preschool PLAY POINTER

Young children look up to "bigger and stronger" siblings, relatives, or superstars. This is a great opportunity to remind children that God is the mighty one we can all look up to.

When all children have had a turn, gather them in a circle. Say: **This is hard work, isn't it?** Ask:

• **How do you feel after pushing someone across the room?**

• **How do you think God would feel if he moved someone across the room?**

Say: **God is powerful and strong! There is no one else who is as mighty as God.** Read aloud Jeremiah 32:18b-19a. **The Bible tells us over and over again how mighty and powerful God is. But God doesn't use his power to push boxes. God uses his power to do great things—like help us, protect us, create the entire world, and love us. Flex your mighty muscles, and let's tell God how great he is!**

Flex your muscles, and have children shout, "Our God is mighty!"

A Mighty Fortress

GROWING CLOSER: No one is as strong as God.

KEY VERSE: "O Lord, my strength and my fortress, my refuge in time of distress" (Jeremiah 16:19a).

SUPPLIES: a Bible, blocks, boxes, blankets, cardboard, crayons

The Game:

Ask: • **Where do you go when you're afraid? Why?**

Say: **The Bible talks about a strong place called a fortress, where people would go when they were afraid. A fortress was a strong tower—kind of like a castle. Let's see what the Bible says about a fortress.**

Read Jeremiah 16:19a from an easy-to-understand Bible translation. Ask:

• **How is God like a strong fortress?**

Say: **This verse tells us that God is like a strong, safe place we can go when we're afraid. God wants us to feel secure and protected, as if we were in a mighty castle. To remember that God is our fortress, let's build a fortress right here in our room!**

Preschool
PLAY POINTER

You may want to bring in pictures of castles and real fortresses. Point out to children that, as strong as those buildings appear, they are no match for the power of God!

Help children drape the blankets over tables and chairs, and let them climb inside the "fortress." Ask:

- **Is this a mighty fortress? Why or why not?**
- **What could we do to make it stronger?**

Allow children to stack blocks or sheets of cardboard against the sides of the fortress to make it stronger. You may want to provide crayons so children can draw stones on the cardboard. Gather everyone inside and ask:

- **Now is this a mighty fortress? Why or why not?**
- **Who would be able to tear down our fortress?**

Say: **We can't make a fortress that is as strong as God. God is powerful and will use his power to protect us. Let's say our verse out loud to remember our powerful God.**

Lead children in saying, "O Lord, my strength and my fortress."

Champion Challenge

GROWING CLOSER: God can do anything.

KEY VERSE: "For nothing is impossible with God" (Luke 1:37).

SUPPLIES: a Bible, jars of food with tight-fitting lids, pails full of rocks and sand, a large box of wooden blocks, a sack of potatoes, a gallon of water in a sealed jug

The Game:

Before children arrive, set up several stations where children can try difficult tasks. You might set out new jars of food (such as jelly or baby food) for them to open, pails of rocks or sand for them to lift, a box for them to fill with blocks and lift, or sacks of potatoes and jugs of water for them to carry. Make sure that at least one station is impossible for them to do.

Say: **I have a muscle challenge for you today. Take a few minutes and try the jobs at these stations. We'll see how strong and powerful you are.** Explain what children are to do at each station, then let children choose which stations they'd like to try. After a few minutes, gather children and ask:

- **Were any of these jobs too hard for you to do?**
- **What was it like to try such hard jobs?**
- **Do you think God could do all these jobs? Why or why not?**

Say: **Let me read a verse that tells about God's power.** Read aloud Luke 1:37, then continue: **This verse tells us that God is all-powerful. Nothing is too hard for God. There is no one who is as powerful as our God.** Ask:

• **How does it feel to know that our God is super powerful?**

Say: **It's good to know that God is so powerful that nothing is too hard for him. God is strong enough to take care of us—no matter what hard things we have to do!**

Big, Big Behemoth

GROWING CLOSER: God is powerful.

KEY VERSE: "Look at the behemoth...what strength he has in his loins, what power in the muscles of his belly...yet his Maker can approach him with his sword" (Job 40:15-16,19).

SUPPLIES: large balloons, large plastic trash bags, audiocassette of upbeat praise music (optional), cassette player (optional)

The Game:

Before children arrive, blow up and tie off at least six or seven balloons per child. Scatter the balloons around the room.

Gather children in a circle and ask:

• **What is the strongest animal you can think of?**

• **Why do you think that animal is so strong?**

• **What would you do if you came face to face with that mighty animal?**

Say: **Let's play a game where we'll make some powerful pretend animals. First, I'll give each person a bag. When I say "Go," you'll run around the room, pick up balloons, and stuff them in your bag. Try to fill your bag so it's big and full. We'll pretend this is your big, powerful animal. Ready?** Distribute plastic bags, then say "Go." You may want to play an audiocassette of upbeat praise music while children are gathering their balloons. When all the balloons have been gathered, help children tie off the bag to make a puffy "animal."

Preschool PLAY POINTER

If you have more than ten children (or don't have the time to blow up many balloons), loosely crumple sheets of newspaper and scatter them around the room.

Ask: • **What big animals did you make?** Children may respond that they made animals such as elephants, crocodiles, or lions.

Say: **The Bible book of Job tells us about a powerful animal called a behemoth. Many people think that the behemoth was probably a hippopotamus or an elephant. Let me read what the Bible tells us about the behemoth.** Read aloud Job 40:15-16, 19, then continue: **The Bible says that God is more powerful than the biggest animal. Pretend that your puffy animal is a mighty behemoth or some other huge and mighty animal. Let's show these animals who's *really* powerful!**

Lead children in tossing their "animals" into the air and shouting, "God is more powerful than *anything!*"

Scripture Index

TEACH YOUR PRESCHOOLERS AS JESUS TAUGHT WITH GROUP'S *HANDS-ON BIBLE CURRICULUM*™

Hands-On Bible Curriculum™ **for preschoolers** helps your preschoolers learn the way they learn best—by touching, exploring, and discovering. With active learning, preschoolers love learning about the Bible, and they really remember what they learn.

Because small children learn best through repetition, Preschoolers and Pre-K & K will learn one important point per lesson, and Toddlers & 2s will learn one point each month with **Hands-On Bible Curriculum**. These important lessons will stick with them and comfort them during their daily lives. Your children will learn:

- •God is our friend,
- •who Jesus is, and
- •we can always trust Jesus.

The **Learning Lab**® is packed with age-appropriate learning tools for fun, faith-building lessons. Toddlers & 2s explore big **Interactive StoryBoards**™ with enticing textures that toddlers love to touch—like sandpaper for earth, cotton for clouds, and blue cellophane for water. While they hear the Bible story, children also *touch* the Bible story. And they learn. **Bible Big Books**™ captivate Preschoolers and Pre-K & K while teaching them important Bible lessons. With **Jumbo Bible Puzzles**™ and involving **Learning Mats**™, your children will see, touch, and explore their Bible stories. Each quarter there's a brand-new collection of supplies to keep your lessons fresh and involving.

Fuzzy, age-appropriate hand puppets are also available to add to the learning experience. What better way to teach your class than with the help of an attention-getting teaching assistant? These child-friendly puppets help you teach each lesson with scripts provided in the **Teacher Guide**. Plus, your children will enjoy teaching the puppets what they learn. Cuddles the Lamb, Whiskers the Mouse, and Pockets the Kangaroo turn each lesson into an interactive and entertaining learning experience.

Just order one **Learning Lab** and one **Teacher Guide** for each age level, add a few common classroom supplies, and presto—you have everything you need to inspire and build faith in your children. For more interactive fun, introduce your children to the age-appropriate puppet who will be your teaching assistant and their friend. No student books are required!

Hands-On Bible Curriculum is also available for elementary grades.